50 Awesome Noodle Recipes

(50 Awesome Noodle Recipes - Volume 1)

Rachel Jones

Content

50 Awesome Noodle Recipes

***

---
1. Beef Stroganoff

Serving: 4 servings | Prep: | Cook: | Ready in: 1hours

Ingredients

- Kosher salt and freshly ground black pepper
- 1 ½ pounds sirloin roast, or beef tenderloin, if you're feeling fancy
- 2 tablespoons all-purpose flour
- 1 ½ teaspoons hot paprika
- 1 tablespoon neutral oil, such as canola or grapeseed
- 4 tablespoons unsalted butter
- ½ pound button mushrooms, cleaned and cut into quarters
- 2 small shallots, thinly sliced
- 12 ounces wide egg noodles
- ¼ cup dry white wine
- 1 cup heavy cream or crème fraîche
- 1 ½ teaspoons Worcestershire sauce
- 1 ½ teaspoons Dijon mustard
- Chopped fresh parsley, for garnish

Direction

- Bring a large pot of salted water to a boil.
- Cut the beef against the grain into 1/2-inch slices, pound lightly, then cut those slices into 1-inch-wide strips.
- Add the flour, paprika, 1 1/2 teaspoons salt and 1 1/2 teaspoons pepper to a large shallow bowl and toss to combine. Dredge the strips of meat in the flour mixture, shake them to remove excess flour, then transfer them to a rimmed baking sheet.

- Place a large skillet over high heat and swirl in the oil. When the oil begins to shimmer, sauté the beef slices, in two batches, until they are well browned on both sides but rare inside, 3 to 4 minutes per batch. Transfer the seared meat to the baking sheet. Turn the heat down slightly.
- Add 1 tablespoon of the butter to the pan. When it has melted and started to foam, add the mushrooms, toss to coat them with the fat, and season with salt and pepper. Cook, stirring frequently, until the mushrooms have released their moisture and are a deep, dark brown, 12 to 15 minutes. About halfway into the process, add the sliced shallots and 1 tablespoon butter and stir to combine.
- While the mushrooms cook, add the noodles to the boiling water, and cook until just done, about 10 minutes. Drain the noodles, and toss with the remaining 2 tablespoons butter. Set aside.
- When the mushrooms and shallots are soft and caramelized, deglaze the pan with the wine, scraping at all the stuck-on bits on the pan's surface. When the wine has reduced by about half, slowly stir in the cream, followed by the Worcestershire and mustard. Add the meat, along with any accumulated juices, and stir to combine. Cook, stirring occasionally, until the dish is hot and the beef is medium-rare, 2 to 3 minutes. Taste, and adjust the seasonings.
- Serve the noodles under or alongside the stroganoff; sprinkle stroganoff with parsley.

---
2. Beef And Broccoli Lo Mein

Serving: 4 servings | Prep: | Cook: | Ready in: 20mins

Ingredients

- 1 (8-ounce) package lo mein noodles
- Salt

- 3 garlic cloves, pressed or minced
- ¼ cup soy sauce
- ¼ cup dark brown sugar
- 2 tablespoons canola or grapeseed oil
- 1 pound chuck or rib steak, thinly sliced against the grain
- 1 (1-inch) piece of ginger, peeled and cut into rounds
- ¼ teaspoon black pepper
- ¼ teaspoon red-pepper flakes
- 1 head broccoli, cut into small florets (about 3 heaping cups)
- 2 carrots, shredded
- 3 scallions or green onions, thinly sliced
- 2 to 3 teaspoons sesame oil (optional)
- 1 lime, cut in wedges, for serving

Direction

- Cook noodles in a large pot of boiling, salted water until tender, about 4 minutes, or according to package instructions. Drain and rinse under cold water. Meanwhile, stir together the garlic, soy sauce and brown sugar, and set aside.
- Heat 1 tablespoon of the oil in a large wok or skillet until hot and shimmering. Add the beef, ginger, black pepper and red-pepper flakes, and cook until crisp on the outside but still pink inside, 2 minutes. Season with salt, and move to a plate.
- Add remaining oil to the wok and heat until shimmering. Add the broccoli and cook, tossing until crisp-tender, 2 minutes. Add 1/4 cup water and steam the broccoli until bright green and some of the liquid has evaporated, 2 minute more. Add the noodles, beef, ginger, carrots and soy sauce mixture to the pan, and toss over medium heat until coated and thickened a little, about 1 to 2 minutes. Salt to taste. Sprinkle with scallions, and drizzle with sesame oil, if using. Toss to coat and serve warm, with lime.

Nutrition Information

- 699: calories;
- 13 grams: monounsaturated fat;
- 7 grams: polyunsaturated fat;
- 67 grams: carbohydrates;
- 35 grams: protein;
- 34 grams: fat;
- 8 grams: dietary fiber;
- 15 grams: sugars;
- 1030 milligrams: sodium;
- 12 grams: saturated fat;
- 2 grams: trans fat;

3. Cannellini Bean Pasta With Beurre Blanc

Serving: 2 servings | Prep: | Cook: | Ready in: 35mins

Ingredients

- 1 (15-ounce) can cannellini beans, rinsed
- 3 cups chicken or vegetable stock
- ¼ cup white wine
- ¼ cup white wine vinegar
- 1 shallot or small white onion, finely chopped
- 3 tablespoons unsalted butter
- 1 cup small pasta, like shells
- Kosher salt and black pepper
- Grated Parmesan, Pecorino Romano or other strong hard cheese, to finish

Direction

- Add the beans and stock to a large pot, and bring to a boil. Turn the heat down, and let simmer for 20 minutes.
- While the beans cook, combine the wine, vinegar, shallot and butter in a small saucepan. Simmer over medium-low for about 15 minutes, shaking the pan as the liquid reduces to keep it from burning. Turn off the heat, and set the beurre blanc aside.
- Stir the pasta into the beans and cook, stirring occasionally, until the pasta is cooked through, about 10 more minutes. Stir in the beurre blanc, and season generously with salt and

pepper. Serve with a little grated cheese on top.

4. Caramelized Scallion Noodles

Serving: 2 servings | Prep: | Cook: | Ready in: 20mins

Ingredients

- Salt
- 6 ounces Chinese broccoli (or other cooking greens), cut into 2-inch pieces
- 10 ounces fresh noodles (or 6 ounces dry pasta)
- 6 tablespoons caramelized-scallion sauce (see recipe), or to taste
- 3 to 4 ounces cooked chicken, ham, tofu, mushrooms or whatever meaty thing you like, sliced, warm
- 2 soft-boiled eggs, halved
- Oyster sauce, to taste
- Soy sauce, to taste
- Raw ginger or spicy pickles of your choice, julienne, for garnish

Direction

- Bring a pot of water to boil, and salt it well. Cook the Chinese broccoli until tender, about 4 minutes. Scoop the greens out with a skimmer, and dry well. Keep the water boiling.
- Cook the noodles according to the package directions. As soon as they're drained, return them to the empty pot, off heat, and dress them with 6 tablespoons of the caramelized-scallion sauce, or to taste. Season with salt, if desired.
- Divide the noodles into bowls, and top with the Chinese broccoli, the chicken (or whatever protein you choose) and the eggs. Drizzle oyster sauce on the Chinese broccoli, and season the eggs with a few drops of soy sauce. Top with a few pinches of julienne ginger or pickles, and serve immediately.

5. Char Kway Teow

Serving: Serves 4 | Prep: | Cook: | Ready in: 15mins

Ingredients

- 3 tablespoons vegetable oil
- ¼ cup chopped garlic
- 3 cups bean sprouts
- 1 pound fresh kway teow (broad rice) noodles
- 1 teaspoon salt
- 1 cup dark soy sauce
- 2 tablespoons seedless tamarind paste dissolved in 3/4 cup water
- 6 large eggs, lightly beaten
- 1 tablespoon Thai chili sauce
- 3 Chinese sausages, thinly sliced
- 8 ounces medium shrimp, peeled and deveined
- 3 ounces chives, sliced into 2-inch pieces

Direction

- Place a large wok or sauté pan over medium heat. When the pan is hot, add 1 tablespoon of the vegetable oil and all of the garlic. Sauté until the garlic is translucent, about 1 minute.
- Add the bean sprouts and noodles to the sauté pan and stir to coat with garlic and oil. Add the salt, soy sauce, tamarind mixture and cup water. Sauté for 1 minute. Transfer to a platter and set aside.
- Return the wok to medium heat. Add the remaining 2 tablespoons vegetable oil. When the oil is hot, add the eggs to the pan and stir until lightly scrambled. Add the noodle mixture, chili sauce and Chinese sausages. Add the shrimp and sauté until they start to turn pink, about 1 minute. Add the chives and toss until the shrimp are fully cooked, about 1 minute more. Serves 4. All recipes adapted from Fatty Crab.

Nutrition Information

- 788: calories;
- 36 grams: protein;
- 4338 milligrams: sodium;
- 24 grams: fat;
- 5 grams: sugars;
- 0 grams: trans fat;
- 13 grams: monounsaturated fat;
- 105 grams: carbohydrates;

6. Chile Oil Noodles With Cilantro

Serving: 4 servings | Prep: | Cook: | Ready in: 20mins

Ingredients

- 14 ounces dried udon noodles
- ¼ cup chile oil with crunchy garlic
- 2 tablespoons pure sesame oil
- 2 teaspoons Sichuan chile oil, or to taste
- 2 teaspoons soy sauce
- ½ cup finely sliced garlic chives or scallions, plus more for garnish
- 2 tablespoons store-bought fried shallots, crumbled by hand (optional)
- ½ cup finely chopped cilantro (see Note), plus a few sprigs for garnish

Direction

- Bring a large pot of water to boil and cook noodles according to package instructions, stirring from time to time to prevent them from sticking. Drain well in a colander, then run noodles under cold water until cooled.
- Meanwhile, in a large bowl, combine all three oils with the soy sauce and 1/2 cup garlic chives.
- Toss cooled noodles into the chile oil mixture. Gently fold in the crumbled fried shallots and chopped cilantro. Divide among four bowls, and top with more garlic chives and cilantro sprigs.

7. Cold Noodles With Chile Oil And Citrusy Cabbage

Serving: 4 to 8 servings | Prep: | Cook: | Ready in: 35mins

Ingredients

- For the noodles:
- ½ cup canola or grapeseed oil
- 1 tablespoon fennel seed
- 1 tablespoon red-pepper flakes
- 2 garlic cloves, very finely chopped
- 1 tablespoon Sichuan peppercorns (optional)
- 1 star anise (optional)
- 1 pound udon, soba or rice noodles, or spaghetti
- 2 tablespoons rice wine vinegar, or fresh lemon or lime juice
- Kosher salt and ground pepper
- For the citrusy cabbage (optional):
- ½ head red cabbage, very thinly sliced
- Kosher salt and ground pepper
- ¼ cup fresh lemon and-or lime juice
- 1 tablespoon finely grated lemon and-or lime zest
- 2 tablespoons olive oil
- For the herby tahini sauce (optional):
- ⅓ cup tahini
- 1 garlic clove, finely grated
- 2 tablespoons fresh lemon or lime juice
- 1 tablespoon sesame oil
- 1 cup parsley and-or cilantro, tender leaves and stems, very finely chopped
- Kosher salt and ground pepper
- For the lemony scallions (optional):
- 1 bunch scallions, very thinly sliced
- ¼ cup olive oil
- 2 tablespoons fresh lemon or lime juice
- 1 tablespoon finely grated lemon or lime zest
- 1 tablespoon soy sauce
- Kosher salt and ground pepper
- More spicy things: Jarred pickled chiles, pickled jalapeños, Calabrian chiles — anything of the sort that will (lightly) set your mouth on fire are welcomed here.

- Toasted seeds or nuts: Toast sesame seeds, chopped peanuts or almonds in a dry skillet until golden brown and toss with a little oil and salt; sprinkle over everything.

Direction

- Heat oil, fennel seed, pepper flakes, garlic, Sichuan peppercorns and star anise (if using) in a small pot over the lowest heat possible. Cook, swirling occasionally, until you start to hear and see the garlic and spices frizzle and toast in the oil, 5 to 8 minutes. (Every stove is different and sometimes the low isn't as low as we'd like, so keep an eye on things; it may take less time.) Keep cooking at the lowest heat setting until the spices are toasted and the garlic is golden brown, another 3 to 5 minutes. Remove from heat and set aside.
- Meanwhile, cook noodles in a large pot of salted water until al dente. Drain and rinse under cold water to stop the cooking. (If not using right away, spread onto a rimmed baking sheet and toss with a little canola oil to prevent sticking.)
- If serving the citrusy cabbage, place cabbage in a large bowl and season with salt and pepper. Add citrus juice and zest, tossing to coat. Let sit a few minutes to soften. Drizzle with olive oil before serving.
- If serving the tahini sauce, whisk tahini, garlic, lemon juice, sesame oil and 1/4 cup water in a small bowl until a creamy dressing forms. (Tahini thickness varies greatly from brand to brand; if you need more water to achieve a smooth, creamy dressing, add it by the teaspoonful until you get the desired texture.) Add herbs and season with salt, pepper and more lemon juice, if desired. Alternatively, place all ingredients and 1/4 cup water in the bowl of a food processor and process until a smooth, creamy dressing forms.
- If serving the lemony scallions, combine scallions, olive oil, lemon juice, lemon zest and soy sauce in a small bowl; season with salt and pepper and let sit for at least 5 minutes before serving.

- When ready to eat, toss noodles with vinegar and season with salt and pepper. Spoon chile oil over the noodles, tossing to coat; keep adding the oil until your noodles are evenly coated. (Keep in mind you have other sauces for the noodles, so you're just looking for them to be coated and sufficiently spicy.) Serve any additional chile oil alongside for personal spooning, with the cabbage and other sauces if you like. See the notes for adding more spicy things and blanched or roasted vegetables.

8. Cold Noodles With Sesame Sauce, Chicken And Cucumbers

Serving: 4 servings | Prep: | Cook: | Ready in: 30mins

Ingredients

- Salt
- 1 to 2 cups shredded cooked chicken or about 8 ounces boneless chicken breast
- 1 pound cucumber
- 12 ounces long pasta like linguine, or 16 ounces fresh Chinese egg noodles
- 2 tablespoons dark sesame oil
- ½ cup sesame paste (tahini) or peanut butter
- 2 tablespoons sugar
- 3 tablespoons soy sauce, or to taste
- 1 teaspoon minced ginger, optional
- 1 tablespoon rice or wine vinegar
- Hot sesame oil or Tabasco sauce to taste
- ½ teaspoon freshly ground black pepper, or more
- At least 1/2 cup minced scallions for garnish

Direction

- Set a large pot of water to boil and salt it. If your chicken is uncooked, poach it in water as it comes to a boil; it will cook in about 10 minutes. Meanwhile, peel cucumbers, cut them in half, and, using a spoon, scoop out seeds. Cut cucumber into shreds and set aside.

- When water comes to a boil, cook pasta until tender but not mushy. (If chicken is not done, you can still add pasta; remove chicken when it is done.) While pasta is cooking, whisk together sesame oil and paste, sugar, soy, ginger, vinegar, hot oil and pepper in a large bowl. Thin sauce with hot water, so that it is about the consistency of heavy cream; you will need 1/4 to 1/2 cup. Stir in cucumber. When pasta is done, drain it and run pasta (and chicken, if necessary) under cold water. Drain. Shred chicken (the easiest way to do this is with your fingers).
- Toss noodles and chicken with sauce and cucumbers. Taste and adjust seasoning as necessary (the dish may need salt), then garnish and serve.

Nutrition Information

- 672: calories;
- 12 grams: sugars;
- 32 grams: protein;
- 6 grams: saturated fat;
- 65 grams: carbohydrates;
- 0 grams: trans fat;
- 14 grams: monounsaturated fat;
- 10 grams: polyunsaturated fat;
- 2 grams: dietary fiber;
- 736 milligrams: sodium;
- 33 grams: fat;

---

9. Cold Pork Rice Noodles With Cucumber And Peanuts

Serving: 4 servings | Prep: | Cook: | Ready in: 25mins

Ingredients

- 3 tablespoons peanut, canola or grapeseed oil
- 6 garlic cloves, pressed or minced
- 1 pound ground pork
- ½ teaspoon black pepper
- 6 tablespoons fish sauce

- 4 tablespoons brown sugar
- 1 to 2 teaspoons sriracha or chile garlic sauce, plus more for serving
- Kosher salt
- 1 (8.8-ounce) package rice vermicelli
- 4 small Persian or hothouse cucumbers, thinly sliced (about 4 ounces)
- 1 small bunch mint, leaves picked (about 1 cup)
- 1 small bunch Thai basil or regular basil, leaves picked (about 1 cup)
- ½ cup roasted peanuts, roughly chopped
- 2 limes, cut in wedges, for serving

Direction

- Heat the oil in a large skillet or wok over medium heat. Add the garlic, pork and black pepper and stir to brown evenly, 2 to 3 minutes. Add fish sauce, sugar and sriracha, and continue cooking until pork is just cooked through and evenly coated with sauce, 2 to 3 minutes more. Set aside.
- Bring a large pot of salted water to a rolling boil. Add the rice noodles and cook until tender, 2 to 4 minutes. Drain and rinse with cold water.
- Drain the sauce off the pork into a bowl, and toss it with the noodles to coat. Divide the dressed noodles across four bowls and top with pork, cucumber, herbs and peanuts (or toss all together and transfer to a bowl). Drizzle with sriracha to taste and serve with lime for squeezing.

Nutrition Information

- 788: calories;
- 44 grams: fat;
- 11 grams: sugars;
- 68 grams: carbohydrates;
- 17 grams: monounsaturated fat;
- 12 grams: polyunsaturated fat;
- 5 grams: dietary fiber;
- 30 grams: protein;
- 2311 milligrams: sodium;

10. Cold Soba Noodles With Dipping Sauce

Serving: 2 to 4 servings | Prep: | Cook: |Ready in: 30mins

Ingredients

- Salt
- 1 cup dashi or chicken stock
- ¼ cup soy sauce
- 2 tablespoons mirin or 1 tablespoon honey mixed with 1 tablespoon water
- 8 ounces soba noodles
- Finely grated or minced ginger,
- Minced scallions or toasted sesame seeds for garnish

Direction

- Bring a large pot of water to a boil, and salt it. Cook noodles until tender but not mushy. Drain, and quickly rinse under cold running water until cold. Drain well.
- Combine dashi or stock, soy sauce and mirin. Taste, and add a little more soy if the flavor is not strong enough. Serve noodles with garnishes, with sauce on side for dipping (or spooning over).

Nutrition Information

- 233: calories;
- 1 gram: sugars;
- 0 grams: dietary fiber;
- 46 grams: carbohydrates;
- 11 grams: protein;
- 1411 milligrams: sodium;

11. Cold Spicy Kimchi Noodles

Serving: 4 to 6 servings | Prep: | Cook: |Ready in: 30mins

Ingredients

- For the dressing:
- 1 cup finely chopped kimchi, plus 2 tablespoons kimchi juice
- 1 medium garlic clove, grated
- 2 teaspoons grated ginger
- 2 tablespoons brown sugar
- 1 tablespoon gochujang (Korean hot pepper paste)
- 1 tablespoon Japanese red miso
- 1 tablespoon sesame oil
- 1 tablespoon rice vinegar
- 2 tablespoons lime juice
- 1 teaspoon orange zest
- 1 teaspoon fish sauce
- ½ teaspoon gochugaru (Korean red pepper flakes)
- Salt
- For the noodles:
- 8 ounces flat rice noodles or soba noodles
- 1 medium cucumber, peeled, halved and sliced into half-moons (about 1 cup)
- 1 cup halved cherry tomatoes
- 3 or 4 large red radishes, sliced into thin rounds
- ½ cup scallions, slivered
- 1 serrano chile, thinly sliced (optional)
- 3 eggs, boiled for 7 minutes, cooled in ice water, peeled and halved (cook 9 minutes for a firmer yolk)
- 2 tablespoons toasted sesame seeds
- Cilantro sprigs or chopped cilantro, for garnish
- Lime wedges, for serving

Direction

- Make the sauce: Put the kimchi, juice, garlic, ginger, brown sugar, gochujang, miso, sesame oil, rice vinegar, lime juice, orange zest, fish sauce and gochugaru in a mixing bowl, and stir well to combine. Taste and adjust salt. Let stand at room temperature for at least 10 minutes (or you can store overnight in the fridge, covered).

- Bring a large pot of generously salted water to a boil. Add noodles and cook for about 5 minutes, or until cooked through but still firm. Drain in a colander, transfer to a bowl of cold water to cool, then drain again and set aside, covered with a towel.
- Just before serving, put noodles in a large mixing bowl. Add the sauce, along with cucumber, tomatoes, radishes, scallions and chile (if using) and toss gently to coat. Divide among individual serving bowls. Top each bowl with a halved egg, sesame seeds, cilantro and a squeeze of lime juice.

Nutrition Information

- 255: calories;
- 3 grams: dietary fiber;
- 467 milligrams: sodium;
- 7 grams: protein;
- 0 grams: trans fat;
- 2 grams: polyunsaturated fat;
- 41 grams: carbohydrates;
- 6 grams: sugars;
- 1 gram: saturated fat;

---

12. Crunchy Noodle Kugel À La Great Aunt Martha

Serving: 8 to 12 servings | Prep: | Cook: | Ready in: 1hours

Ingredients

- 1 cup raisins
- Sherry or orange juice
- 1 pound egg noodles
- 6 tablespoons unsalted butter, cut into pieces, more for pan
- 4 large eggs

- 3 cups cottage cheese
- 1 cup sour cream
- ⅓ cup sugar
- 1 teaspoon ground cinnamon
- Grated zest of 1 lemon
- Pinch of salt

Direction

- Put raisins in a microwave-safe bowl or small saucepan and cover with sherry or orange juice. Heat on stove top or in microwave oven until liquid is steaming hot (about 1 1/2 minutes in microwave or 3 minutes on stove). Let cool while you prepare kugel mixture.
- Preheat oven to 400 degrees. Butter an 11-by-17-inch jellyroll pan. Cook noodles according to package directions and drain well. Immediately return noodles to pot and add butter. Toss until butter melts.
- In a large bowl, whisk together the eggs, cottage cheese, sour cream, sugar, cinnamon, lemon zest and salt. Drain raisins and add to bowl along with buttered noodles. Mix well.
- Spread mixture in prepared pan and smooth top. Bake until top is crusty and golden, 25 to 35 minutes. Serve warm or at room temperature.

Nutrition Information

- 446: calories;
- 18 grams: protein;
- 5 grams: monounsaturated fat;
- 326 milligrams: sodium;
- 9 grams: saturated fat;
- 0 grams: trans fat;
- 2 grams: dietary fiber;
- 54 grams: carbohydrates;
- 19 grams: sugars;

13. Curry Noodles With Shrimp And Coconut

Serving: 4 to 6 servings | Prep: | Cook: |Ready in: 35mins

Ingredients

- 12 ounces rice noodles (vermicelli)
- ½ teaspoon coriander seeds
- ½ teaspoon cumin seeds
- ½ teaspoon fennel seeds
- 6 allspice berries
- 2 tablespoons coconut oil
- 1 medium onion, finely diced, about 2 cups
- 2 tablespoons finely chopped lemongrass
- ½ teaspoon grated garlic
- 2 teaspoons grated ginger
- Salt and pepper
- 1 ½ teaspoons turmeric
- ⅛ teaspoon cayenne
- Zest and juice of 1 lime
- 1 teaspoon fish sauce
- 2 cups coconut milk
- 1 pound shrimp, peeled and deveined
- 1 pint cherry tomatoes, halved
- ½ cup slivered scallions
- Cilantro, basil and mint leaves, for garnish

Direction

- Cook rice noodles according to package directions, then drain and rinse well with cool water. Set aside. Keep a pot of boiling water on stove for reheating noodles later.
- Toast coriander seeds, cumin seeds, fennel seeds and allspice berries in a dry pan over medium heat until fragrant, then grind in a spice mill or with a mortar and pestle.
- Put coconut oil in a wide skillet over medium heat. Add onions and cook until softened, about 5 to 8 minutes. Add lemongrass, garlic and ginger to softened onions and cook for 2 minutes more.
- Season with salt and pepper, then add ground coriander, cumin, fennel and allspice. Add turmeric, cayenne, lime zest and juice, fish sauce and coconut milk. Simmer gently for 5 minutes.
- Season shrimp and cherry tomatoes with salt. Add to pan and cover until shrimp are cooked, 3 to 4 minutes.
- Dip noodles briefly in hot water to reheat, then drain and divide among bowls. Spoon shrimp, tomatoes and sauce over each serving. Sprinkle with scallions and garnish with cilantro, basil and mint leaves.

Nutrition Information

- 486: calories;
- 1 gram: polyunsaturated fat;
- 57 grams: carbohydrates;
- 735 milligrams: sodium;
- 22 grams: fat;
- 19 grams: saturated fat;
- 0 grams: trans fat;
- 3 grams: sugars;
- 17 grams: protein;

14. Exciting Noodle Kugel

Serving: 6 servings | Prep: | Cook: |Ready in: 45mins

Ingredients

- Butter to grease pan
- 8 ounces medium egg noodles, preferably high-quality pappardelle
- 1 ½ cups cottage cheese (with curds, not creamed or whipped) or farmer cheese
- 1 ½ cups sour cream
- ½ medium onion, finely minced
- 1 clove garlic, chopped
- 1 tablespoon Worcestershire sauce
- Dash of Tabasco sauce
- 1 teaspoon salt, or to taste
- Freshly ground pepper, to taste
- 2 tablespoons grated Parmesan
- ¼ cup chives, sliced

Direction

- Heat oven to 350 degrees. Butter the inside of a 2 or 2 1/2-quart casserole or gratin dish.
- Bring a pot of water to a boil, add the noodles and cook until al dente, about 7 minutes. Drain the noodles, put in a medium bowl, and toss with cottage or farmer cheese, sour cream, onion, garlic, Worcestershire sauce, Tabasco and salt and pepper.
- Spoon into the buttered dish and sprinkle with the Parmesan and chives. Bake until golden and crusty on top, 35 to 40 minutes.

Nutrition Information

- 350: calories;
- 17 grams: fat;
- 0 grams: trans fat;
- 4 grams: monounsaturated fat;
- 2 grams: dietary fiber;
- 404 milligrams: sodium;
- 14 grams: protein;
- 10 grams: saturated fat;
- 1 gram: polyunsaturated fat;
- 34 grams: carbohydrates;
- 5 grams: sugars;

15. Faloodeh (Persian Lime And Rose Water Granita With Rice Noodles)

Serving: 6 to 8 servings | Prep: | Cook: | Ready in: 20mins

Ingredients

- 1 cup granulated sugar
- Fine sea salt
- ⅓ cup lime juice, plus wedges, for serving (about 3 to 4 limes)
- 2 tablespoons rose water
- 4 ounces very thin rice noodles or rice vermicelli

Direction

- Place 1/2 cup water in a small saucepan and set over low heat. Add about half the sugar and stir to dissolve completely. Add 1/8 teaspoon salt and the rest of the sugar and continue stirring until completely dissolved. Take off the heat and let cool to room temperature.
- In a freezer-safe bowl or dish, stir together 4 cups water, cooled syrup, lime juice and rose water, then place in freezer until ice crystals begin to form on the edges of the mixture, about 1 hour.
- In a medium pot, bring 4 quarts water to a boil. Add the noodles and cook thoroughly until there is no bite left, about 8 minutes or as instructed on the package. Drain and rinse immediately with cold water. Use scissors to cut noodles into 1-inch pieces, then stir them into the partly frozen syrup mixture. It's important that the mixture has begun to freeze before adding the noodles so that they don't all sink to the bottom of the dish, so if your syrup mixture needs more time, freeze for another hour before adding noodles.
- Every hour for the next several hours, scrape the granita thoroughly with a fork to prevent huge icy chunks from forming. The mixture should be light and airy, punctuated with crunchy noodles.
- To serve, scrape and serve bowlfuls of faloodeh with lime wedges.

16. Homemade Hamburger Helper

Serving: 4 servings | Prep: | Cook: | Ready in: 1hours15mins

Ingredients

- ¼ cup neutral oil, such as canola or vegetable
- 1 large yellow onion, diced into 1/2-inch pieces
- Kosher salt and black pepper

- 3 garlic cloves, minced
- 5 strips uncooked smoked bacon, finely chopped
- 1 pound ground beef
- 1 cup dry white wine
- 3 cups chicken stock or water
- ¾ cup heavy cream
- ¼ to ⅓ cup hot sauce
- 2 teaspoons hot smoked paprika
- 1 bay leaf
- 8 ounces elbow pasta
- 5 slices American cheese, ripped into small pieces
- 1 ½ cups grated Cheddar
- ½ cup finely chopped chives

Direction

- Heat a large (12-inch) sauté pan or Dutch oven over medium-low heat, and add oil and onion; season lightly with salt and pepper. (The hot sauce added in Step 6 will add a lot of flavor, so be careful not to overseason here.) Let cook until the onions turn light beige in color and begin to caramelize, 20 to 25 minutes.
- Add garlic, and cook until fragrant and starting to brown ever so slightly, about 2 minutes.
- Increase heat to medium-high and add bacon and ground beef, using the back of a large spoon to break up the meat into smaller pieces. Continue to cook until the liquid has mostly evaporated and the meat starts to sear and develop a crust on the bottom of the pan, 12 to 15 minutes.
- Remove pan from the heat and carefully drain off most of the fat, leaving a little in the pan to keep the meat moist.
- Return pan to the medium-high heat and add white wine, allowing it to reduce until the mixture is almost dry, about 10 minutes.
- Add the chicken stock, heavy cream, hot sauce, paprika and bay leaf to the pan. Mix until combined and bring to a boil over medium-high.

- Once the mixture is boiling, add the pasta and cook until al dente, stirring often, about 9 minutes.
- Reduce the heat to low and stir in both types of cheese, stirring until completely melted and sauce is thickened.
- Remove the pan from heat, stir in chives and season to taste with salt and pepper. Serve immediately.

17. Jajangmyeon

Serving: Serves 4 | Prep: | Cook: |Ready in: 1hours

Ingredients

- 2 tablespoons neutral oil, like canola
- 8 ounces pork belly, cut into half-inch dice
- 8 ounce pork shoulder, cut into half-inch dice
- 2 inches of ginger root, peeled and minced
- 4 garlic cloves, peeled and minced
- 1 small carrot, peeled and diced
- 1 large waxy potato, like a Yukon gold, peeled and diced
- 1 Spanish onion, peeled and diced
- 1 zucchini, 1/2 peeled and diced, 1/2 peeled and julienned
- ½ cup chunjang, Korean black-bean paste
- 2 tablespoons light brown sugar
- Kosher salt to taste
- 1 pound fresh udon noodles
- ½ cup pickled yellow daikon radish, cut into half moons

Direction

- Heat a wok or large sauté pan over high heat, and add the oil to it. When it shimmers and is about to smoke, add the pork belly and shoulder, and allow them to brown, stirring occasionally, approximately 5 to 7 minutes.
- Turn the heat to medium-high, and add the ginger and garlic, and sauté until softened, approximately 1 to 2 minutes, then add the carrot, potato, onion and the diced zucchini,

and cook, stirring occasionally, until softened, approximately 5 to 7 minutes.

- Add the black-bean paste to the pan, along with the sugar, a light sprinkle of salt and about 1 cup water. Stir to combine, then allow to cook until the sauce has thickened and the meat and vegetables have cooked through entirely, approximately 15 to 20 minutes.
- Meanwhile, set a large pot filled with water over high heat to bring to a boil. Add the noodles, and cook until they are soft, approximately 6 to 8 minutes. Reserve a cup of the noodle water, and then drain the noodles, rinsing them with cold water to bring them to room temperature. Set aside in a large serving bowl.
- Add a little of the reserved noodle water to the pork-and-black-bean sauce if it is too thick, then pour the sauce over the noodles. Garnish with the julienned zucchini and the pickled daikon.

Nutrition Information

- 996: calories;
- 99 grams: carbohydrates;
- 7 grams: dietary fiber;
- 9 grams: sugars;
- 36 grams: protein;
- 51 grams: fat;
- 16 grams: saturated fat;
- 0 grams: trans fat;
- 8 grams: polyunsaturated fat;
- 23 grams: monounsaturated fat;
- 1008 milligrams: sodium;

---

18. Japanese Style Tuna Noodle Salad

Serving: 4 servings | Prep: | Cook: | Ready in: 30mins

Ingredients

- For the Salad:

- ¼ cup cut dried wakame seaweed
- 8 ounces dried udon noodles (or whatever noodles you have on hand)
- 1 to 2 tablespoons furikake or sesame seeds
- 10 to 12 ounces tuna in oil, drained
- 2 scallions, trimmed and thinly sliced
- For the Dressing:
- 2 tablespoons sesame oil
- 2 tablespoons canola oil
- 2 tablespoons rice wine vinegar
- 1 tablespoon mirin
- 1 tablespoon soy sauce
- 1 teaspoon sweet miso

Direction

- Bring a large pot of water to a boil over high, and set the wakame in a small bowl. Once the water comes to a boil, ladle or pour enough over the wakame to cover it by 2 inches; let the wakame soak for 10 minutes. Transfer the wakame to a colander to drain and cool; set aside.
- While the wakame soaks, cook the noodles according to the package instructions.
- Meanwhile, prepare the dressing: In a measuring cup or bowl, whisk to combine the sesame oil, canola oil, rice wine vinegar, mirin, soy sauce and miso; set aside.
- In a small skillet, lightly toast the sesame seeds, if using, over medium-low heat until fragrant; set aside.
- Drain the cooked noodles in the colander, then transfer to a wide, shallow serving bowl. Add the wakame and about 3/4 of the dressing, and toss to coat. Divide the noodles among 4 bowls. Top each portion with tuna, drizzle with the remaining dressing, then sprinkle with the scallions and furikake or sesame seeds. Serve hot, cold or anywhere in between.

19. Japchae (Korean Glass Noodles)

Serving: 6 to 8 servings | Prep: | Cook: |Ready in: 1hours15mins

Ingredients

- For the beef:
- ½ pound stew beef
- ½ teaspoon sugar
- 1 tablespoon soy sauce
- ¼ teaspoon toasted sesame oil
- 1 clove garlic, smashed
- 1 1 1/2-inch-thick slice peeled ginger, smashed
- Freshly ground black pepper
- For the pickled lotus root (optional):
- 1 pound lotus root, trimmed and peeled
- 1 cup water
- 6 tablespoons soy sauce
- 3 tablespoons rice vinegar
- 3 tablespoons sugar
- For the noodles:
- 1 package (about 1 pound) Korean sweet-potato noodles (also called dangmyeon or Korean glass noodles)
- Fine sea salt
- 1 bunch spinach, stemmed (or 5 ounces baby spinach)
- Grapeseed, canola or other neutral-tasting oil
- 1 bunch scallions, trimmed, halved lengthwise, and cut into 1 1/2-inch strips (about 2 cups)
- 2 medium carrots, julienned into 1 1/2-inch strips (about 2 cups)
- 2 medium red bell peppers, seeded and very thinly sliced (about 2 cups)
- 4 ounces shiitake mushrooms, stemmed and cut into 1/2-inch strips
- 3 cloves garlic, minced
- 1 medium yellow onion, root removed and thinly sliced (about 2 cups)
- 6 tablespoons soy sauce, divided
- ¾ teaspoon toasted sesame oil
- 2 eggs, beaten
- 1 sheet nori, halved and julienned

Direction

- Line three baking sheets with parchment paper. Set aside.
- Cut the beef into 1/2-inch strips. Place in a medium bowl, and add sugar, soy sauce, toasted sesame oil, smashed garlic, ginger and black pepper. Toss well to combine. Set aside for 30 minutes.
- If making pickled lotus root, slice roots into 1/8-inch-thick discs, and place in a medium bowl filled with cold water. Set aside. Place a colander in the sink. Bring 4 quarts of water to a boil in a medium sauce pot. Blanch lotus-root slices for 1 minute, then drain.
- In a medium saucepan, combine 1 cup water, 6 tablespoons soy sauce, 3 tablespoons rice vinegar and 3 tablespoons sugar. Set over medium heat, and bring to a boil, stirring occasionally to ensure sugar dissolves. Cool to room temperature, then pour over cooled lotus root. Set aside.
- Place noodles in a large bowl. Cover with warm tap water, and set aside to soak for 30 minutes.
- Fill a medium pot with 3 quarts water, and bring to a boil. Season with 1 tablespoon salt. Add spinach, and blanch for 10 seconds, then use a spider or tongs to remove to a parchment-lined tray. Spread out into a single layer, and allow to cool, then squeeze out any excess water and chop roughly.
- Fill a large pot with 6 quarts of water, cover, and set over high heat to come to a boil.
- Set a large sauté pan over high heat. Add 1 tablespoon oil. When it shimmers, add scallions and a pinch of salt. Sauté for 2 minutes until they are tender but not completely soft. Transfer to a baking sheet, and spread into a shallow pile to cool quickly.
- Return pan to high heat. Add 1 tablespoon oil. When it shimmers, add carrots and a pinch of salt. Sauté for about 6 minutes until tender but not completely soft. Transfer to sheet with scallions, and spread into another shallow pile to cool quickly. Repeat with bell peppers.
- Return pan to high heat. Add 1 tablespoon oil. When it shimmers, add shiitakes, and cook until lightly caramelized, about 3 minutes.

Move mushrooms to the edges of the pan, add 1 teaspoon oil to the center of the pan and add garlic. Turn off heat and allow garlic to gently sizzle for about 10 seconds, then stir garlic into mushrooms to prevent it from taking on any color. Transfer to second parchment-lined baking sheet and allow to cool, then squeeze out any extra water.

- Return pan to high heat. Add 1 tablespoon oil. When it shimmers, add onions and a pinch of salt. Sauté for about 8 minutes until lightly caramelized and translucent, but still a little crunchy within. Transfer to sheet with mushrooms and spread into another shallow pile to cool quickly.
- Return pan to high heat. Add 1 tablespoon oil. When it shimmers, add beef and sauté for about 3 minutes, until meat is tender and barely cooked through and just starting to caramelize. Transfer to sheet with onions, and spread out to cool quickly.
- Set a colander in the sink. Add 3 tablespoons soy sauce to large pot of boiling water. Add noodles and cook for 4 minutes until tender, then drain into colander, rinsing with cold water. When noodles are warm but not hot, drain and transfer to a large bowl. If noodles are unmanageably long, use kitchen shears to shorten them. Add 3 tablespoons soy sauce, ¾ teaspoon toasted sesame oil, ¼ teaspoon salt and freshly ground black pepper. Toss to coat evenly.
- Add all the vegetables and beef to the noodles. Toss thoroughly with hands to ensure everything is evenly distributed. Taste and adjust seasoning with soy sauce, sesame oil and salt as needed. Transfer to serving dish.
- Set a large nonstick pan over medium heat, and add 1 teaspoon oil. Add eggs and reduce heat to low. Cook into a thin omelet, flipping before it takes on any color. Turn omelet out onto a cutting board, and julienne into thin strips.
- Garnish noodles with egg and nori strips and lotus root, if using. Serve at room temperature.

Serving: 2 servings as a main course or 4 as a side | Prep: | Cook: | Ready in: 20mins

Ingredients

- Kosher salt, to taste
- ¼ cup extra-virgin olive oil, plus more for serving
- 2 cloves garlic, smashed flat and peeled
- 1 pound lacinato kale, thick ribs removed
- Freshly ground black pepper, to taste
- ½ pound pasta, like pappardelle or rigatoni
- ¾ cup coarsely grated Parmigiano- Reggiano

Direction

- Put a large pot of generously salted water over high heat, and bring to a boil. In a small skillet over medium heat, add olive oil and garlic, and cook until the garlic begins to sizzle. Reduce heat to low, and cook very gently until garlic is soft and begins to turn light gold, about 5 minutes. Remove from heat.
- When water is boiling, add kale leaves, and cook until tender, but not mushy, about 5 minutes. Pull out the hot, dripping kale leaves with tongs, and put directly into a blender. (Don't drain the pot; you'll use that same boiling water to cook the pasta.) Add garlic and its oil to the blender, along with a splash of hot water from the pot if you need some more liquid to get the blender going. Blend into a fine, thick green purée. Taste, and adjust seasoning with salt and pepper, then blend again.
- Add the pasta to the still-boiling water, and cook according to directions on the package. Ladle out about a cup of the water to save for finishing the dish, then drain the pasta and return it to the dry pot. Add the kale purée, about 3/4 of the grated cheese and a splash of the reserved pasta water. Toss until all the pasta is well coated and bright green, adding another splash of pasta water if needed so that

17

the sauce is loose and almost creamy in texture. Serve in bowls right away, and top with an extra drizzle of olive oil and the rest of the grated cheese.

Nutrition Information

- 944: calories;
- 42 grams: fat;
- 5 grams: polyunsaturated fat;
- 108 grams: carbohydrates;
- 962 milligrams: sodium;
- 11 grams: saturated fat;
- 23 grams: monounsaturated fat;
- 12 grams: dietary fiber;
- 9 grams: sugars;
- 40 grams: protein;

21. Khao Soi Gai (Northern Thai Coconut Curry Noodles With Chicken)

Serving: 4 servings | Prep: | Cook: | Ready in: 4hours

Ingredients

- For the curry paste:
- 3 dried red Thai chiles (or chiles de árbol)
- 2 fresh or dried makrut lime leaves (optional)
- 15 cilantro stems with leaves (about 1/4 bunch)
- 2 large shallots or 1 medium yellow onion, roughly chopped
- 2 (1 1/2- to 2-inch) pieces fresh, unpeeled turmeric, scrubbed and roughly chopped (or 2 tablespoons ground turmeric)
- 1 (4-inch) piece lemongrass, from the base of the stalk, sliced
- 1 (3-inch) piece fresh ginger, peeled and roughly chopped
- 4 large garlic cloves, peeled and smashed
- 1 teaspoon curry powder

- 1 teaspoon shrimp paste or 2 teaspoons fish sauce (optional)
- ½ teaspoon grated lime zest (preferably from a fresh makrut lime)
- For the noodles:
- 3 cups neutral oil
- 1 (16-ounce) package dried, flat Chinese-style egg noodles, or dried tagliatelle pasta nests
- Kosher salt
- For the chicken and broth:
- 2 (13-ounce) cans full-fat coconut milk (not shaken or stirred)
- 2 cups chicken broth (preferably low-sodium)
- Kosher salt
- 8 chicken leg drumsticks (about 2 pounds)
- 2 to 4 tablespoons fish sauce
- 2 to 4 tablespoons palm sugar or brown sugar
- For serving:
- ½ cup homemade or store-bought Yunnanese-style pickled mustard greens, for serving
- 1 shallot, peeled and thinly sliced, for serving
- Chile paste or chile oil, for serving
- Lime wedges, for serving

Direction

- Make the curry paste: Bring 1/4 cup of water to a boil in a small saucepan. Add the dried chiles and makrut lime leaves (if using) to a small bowl; pour the boiling water on top and let steep for 10 minutes.
- While the mixture steeps, separate the cilantro leaves from the stems; set leaves and any tender stems aside for garnish. Roughly chop cilantro stems and add to a small food processor (or the bowl of a large mortar and pestle) along with the shallots, turmeric, lemongrass, ginger, garlic, curry powder, shrimp paste (if using) and lime zest.
- Add the soaked chile mixture (including its liquid) and process (or crush with a pestle) until curry paste is smooth, scraping down sides of bowl as needed, about 10 minutes for either method. Curry paste can be made up to 2 weeks ahead; store in a covered container in the refrigerator.

- Prepare the fried noodles: In a medium (2-quart) saucepan, bring 3 cups neutral oil to 325 degrees over medium-high heat. Add 4 ounces noodles and fry, flipping once or twice, until light brown, 30 to 60 seconds. Using a slotted spoon, transfer noodles to a paper towel-lined plate; set aside until ready to serve. Cool, strain and store remaining oil in a covered jar for another use.
- Heat a large Dutch oven or pot over medium. Add about 1/4 cup coconut cream, scraped from the top of one of the cans of coconut milk, to the pot and let it melt, about 10 seconds. Add at least half of the curry paste — or more, for a more pungent khao soi — and stir until deeply fragrant, about 30 seconds. Add 1 1/2 cups chicken broth and the remaining coconut milk, and increase heat to medium-high. Bring mixture just to a low boil, about 3 minutes.
- Use 1 tablespoon salt to season drumsticks, then add them to the boiling curry mixture. Cover, and let simmer until chicken is cooked through, 20 to 30 minutes. Uncover, lower heat, and add remaining 1/2 cup chicken stock along with 1 cup water. (It should be more like soup than stew.) Season to taste with fish sauce, sugar and salt. Turn heat to very low, and cover to keep warm.
- Meanwhile, bring 4 quarts water to a boil in a large pot. Add 2 teaspoons salt and remaining 12 ounces noodles. Cook until al dente. Drain and portion into four bowls. Add 2 drumsticks to each bowl, and about 2 cups curry broth. Garnish with fried noodles, pickled mustard greens, sliced shallots, chile paste or oil, reserved cilantro leaves and lime wedges. Serve immediately.

22. Kimchi Noodle Cake

Serving: 4 servings | Prep: | Cook: | Ready in: 30mins

Ingredients

- ½ pound rice noodles, fettuccine width
- Salt and pepper
- 1 cup kimchi, any kind, squeezed dry and roughly chopped
- 1 tablespoon dried shrimp, chopped
- ½ cup chopped scallions or Korean chives
- ¼ cup Korean red pepper paste (gochujang)
- 1 teaspoon toasted sesame oil
- 1 tablespoon toasted sesame seeds
- 2 tablespoons vegetable oil
- 3 eggs, lightly beaten
- Cilantro sprigs, for garnish

Direction

- Put rice noodles in a bowl and cover with boiling water. Let soak until softened, about 10 minutes, then rinse with cold water and drain well. Transfer noodles to a mixing bowl. Season lightly with salt and pepper.
- Add kimchi, dried shrimp, scallions, gochujang, sesame oil and sesame seeds to bowl and toss well to coat.
- Set a heavy 12-inch skillet over medium-high heat. Add vegetable oil and heat until wavy. Slip in noodle mixture and cover. Turn heat to medium and cook for 5 minutes, until bottom is browned and crisp.
- Season eggs with salt and pepper and pour over noodles. Tilt skillet to distribute eggs evenly over bottom of pan. Cover and cook until eggs are just set, 4 to 5 minutes. Invert cake onto a cutting board or round platter. Let cool slightly, then cut into wedges, garnish with cilantro and serve.

Nutrition Information

- 192: calories;
- 0 grams: trans fat;
- 3 grams: dietary fiber;
- 10 grams: carbohydrates;
- 8 grams: protein;
- 809 milligrams: sodium;
- 14 grams: fat;
- 2 grams: sugars;

- 7 grams: monounsaturated fat;

23. Lemony Pasta With Asparagus And White Beans

Serving: 4 to 6 servings | Prep: | Cook: | Ready in: 30mins

Ingredients

- 1 large lemon, plus more fresh lemon juice for serving
- 1 (15-ounce) can white beans, rinsed
- 1 shallot, finely diced, or 2 tablespoons finely diced red onion
- 3 garlic cloves (2 thinly sliced, 1 finely grated)
- ¼ teaspoon red-pepper flakes, plus more to taste
- Kosher salt
- 4 tablespoons extra-virgin olive oil
- 1 pound short pasta, such as campanelle, fusilli or farfalle
- 2 bunches asparagus (about 2 pounds), ends trimmed, stalks sliced into 1/2-inch pieces
- ⅔ cup coarsely chopped Italian parsley leaves
- ½ cup grated Parmesan, plus more for serving
- Black pepper

Direction

- Grate the zest from the lemon into a small bowl. Halve the lemon and squeeze the juice from half of it on top of the zest. Add the white beans, shallot or onion, grated garlic, red-pepper flakes and a large pinch of salt and toss well. Drizzle in 1 tablespoon olive oil and set aside.
- Bring a large pot of heavily salted water to a boil. Add pasta and cook until just shy of al dente, usually 2 minutes less than the package directs.
- Meanwhile, heat a 12-inch sauté pan over medium-high heat. When hot, add the remaining 3 tablespoons oil, then add the asparagus. Sauté until the asparagus is tender

and starting to brown at the edges, 7 to 10 minutes. Add a big pinch of salt and the sliced garlic and sauté until the garlic is lightly golden, 1 to 2 minutes longer.
- Dip a coffee mug or glass measuring cup into the pasta water and scoop out about 1/2 cup of it to use for the sauce. Drain pasta, shaking it well. Add pasta, bean mixture, parsley and Parmesan to sauté pan and cook until the beans are hot and the pasta is al dente. If the mixture looks dry, splash in some (or all) of the reserved pasta water. Squeeze remaining lemon half over pasta, toss and taste. Season with pepper; add more salt, red-pepper flakes and lemon juice, if desired.

24. Mac And Queso Fundido

Serving: 4 servings | Prep: | Cook: | Ready in: 30mins

Ingredients

- Kosher salt and freshly ground black pepper
- 1 tablespoon vegetable or canola oil
- 5 ounces mushrooms, preferably cremini, sliced (about 2 cups)
- ¼ pound fresh chorizo or hot Italian sausage, casing removed (optional)
- 8 ounces cavatappi (corkscrew) or other small pasta
- 2 tablespoons unsalted butter
- 4 garlic cloves, minced
- 3 tablespoons all-purpose flour
- 1 cup chicken stock, vegetable stock or water
- ¾ cup milk
- ¼ cup heavy cream
- 1 teaspoon onion powder
- ½ teaspoon smoked paprika
- 1 ½ cups shredded mozzarella
- 1 cup shredded Mexican cheese blend
- ½ cup shredded Parmesan
- Sliced scallions, for serving

Direction

- Bring a large pot of well-salted water to a boil over high heat for the pasta.
- As the water comes to a boil, heat the vegetable oil in a large skillet over medium. Add the mushrooms and cook until crispy and golden brown all over, about 5 minutes on each side. Season with a pinch of salt and pepper, and transfer to a plate. Wipe out the skillet.
- Line another plate with paper towels. Add the chorizo to the skillet and cook, crumbling the meat with a spatula, until the fat has rendered and the chorizo is crispy, 10 to 12 minutes. Remove and set aside on the paper towels to drain.
- Drop the pasta into the boiling water and cook according to the package directions. Drain and return the pasta back to the pot.
- Meanwhile, in the skillet, melt the butter over medium heat. Stir in the garlic and cook for 2 minutes. Whisk in the flour, then slowly whisk in the stock. Once the stock is incorporated, whisk in the milk and cream until smooth. Whisk in onion powder and smoked paprika, then cook until the mixture begins to thicken, about 3 minutes. Remove from the heat and stir in the mozzarella, Mexican cheese blend and Parmesan until completely melted. Adjust the salt to taste.
- Add the cheese sauce to the pasta and stir to evenly coat the pasta in the sauce. Leave in the pot or transfer to a serving dish and top with the mushrooms and chorizo, if using. Garnish with scallions and serve immediately.

25. Mee Goreng (Southeast Asian Fried Noodles)

Serving: 6 servings | Prep: | Cook: | Ready in: 30mins

Ingredients

- 1 pound fresh yellow egg noodles (such as hokkien mee, yakisoba or lo mein)
- 1 ½ cups sambal tumis (see recipe)
- 2 tablespoons canola oil
- 1 pound shrimp, peeled and deveined, tails intact
- 1 cup cubed fried tofu puffs or firm tofu in 1/2 inch chunks
- 3 small bok choy, ends trimmed, chopped
- Kosher salt, to taste
- 1 ½ cups fresh bean sprouts
- 2 tomatoes, cut into wedges
- Sweet soy sauce (kecap manis), to taste
- 2 limes, cut into wedges (if available, calamansi are best)
- Dried shallots or fried onions, to taste
- Red Serrano or Fresno chiles, thinly sliced, for serving

Direction

- Cook noodles according to package instructions.
- Heat prepared sambal tumis in a wok or large skillet for about 5 minutes over medium heat. Add cooked noodles, tofu or tofu puffs and bok choy and stir to make sure everything is mixed with the sambal. (If the noodles start to stick together, add a splash or two of water until they loosen.)
- Heat the canola oil in a large frying pan over medium heat. Add the shrimp; season with salt and cook for about 5 minutes, or until pink and opaque. Transfer shrimp and any juices to the sambal mixture in the wok; add the tomato wedges, bean sprouts and a drizzle of sweet soy sauce to taste. Stir for 1 minute over medium heat, and season with salt to taste.
- Remove the lemongrass, heap the mee goreng onto a platter and serve immediately, or at room temperature, with lime wedges, sliced red Serrano or Fresno chiles and dried shallots or fried onions.

Nutrition Information

- 492: calories;
- 13 grams: fat;
- 5 grams: polyunsaturated fat;

- 67 grams: carbohydrates;
- 30 grams: protein;
- 2 grams: saturated fat;
- 0 grams: trans fat;
- 7 grams: sugars;
- 955 milligrams: sodium;

26. Parsleyed Noodles

Serving: 6 servings | Prep: | Cook: | Ready in: 10mins

Ingredients

- 1 pound wide egg noodles, cooked according to package directions and drained
- ¼ cup melted butter
- Salt and freshly ground black pepper to taste
- ¼ cup finely chopped parsley

Direction

- Combine all the ingredients, in a large serving dish, toss gently and serve.

Nutrition Information

- 360: calories;
- 11 grams: protein;
- 6 grams: saturated fat;
- 0 grams: trans fat;
- 3 grams: dietary fiber;
- 1 gram: sugars;
- 54 grams: carbohydrates;
- 204 milligrams: sodium;

27. Pasta Tahdig

Serving: 6 to 8 servings | Prep: | Cook: | Ready in: 1hours

Ingredients

- Salt

- 1 pound spaghetti or capellini (angel hair)
- Extra-virgin olive oil
- 2 cups tomato sauce
- 1 cup finely grated Parmesan, plus more for serving
- Optional: 1 tablespoon Calabrian chile paste or 1 teaspoon red-pepper flakes

Direction

- Bring a large pot of generously salted water to a boil over high heat. Set a colander in the sink. Cook the pasta, stirring occasionally with tongs to prevent clumping. Taste, and adjust salt as needed. When the pasta is al dente, drain into colander.
- Return pasta to pot, and add 2 tablespoons oil, tomato sauce, 1 cup Parmesan and chile paste or flakes, if using. Stir well with tongs to combine. and taste to ensure that the mixture is well seasoned.
- Preheat a 10-inch nonstick pan over medium heat. Add 3 tablespoons oil. When it shimmers, pile in the pasta, and use a silicone spatula to lightly pat it evenly down into the pan. The pan may seem perilously full, but the cake will condense as it cooks. Use spatula to gently coax the pasta on the edges into a cakelike shape, and reduce heat to medium low. Add oil as needed until you can see it gently bubbling up the sides of the pan — this will ensure that the edges of the tahdig are brown.
- Cook, rotating pan a quarter-turn every 5 minutes to ensure even browning. Periodically run spatula around the edges to prevent sticking. After 20 minutes, carefully tip excess oil into a heatproof bowl, then cover the pan with a pizza pan or large, flat pot lid. Carefully flip tahdig onto pan.
- Add oil back into pan, and return to medium heat. If needed, add more oil to coat bottom of the pan. Carefully slide tahdig back into pan, using spatula to coax it back into shape. When oil begins to gently bubble up the sides of the pan, reduce heat to medium low, and cook for

20 minutes, rotating pan a quarter-turn every 5 minutes.

- Wipe pizza pan clean, tip out excess oil and flip tahdig onto pan as before. If either side (or both) can use a little more crisping, return tahdig to pan without oil, increase heat to medium high and cook for 60-90 seconds, until sizzling and properly browned.
- Dab away any excess grease with a paper towel. Allow tahdig to cool for 10 minutes before using a sharp bread knife to cut into slices. Serve warm or at room temperature with grated Parmesan.

Nutrition Information

- 296: calories;
- 6 grams: fat;
- 3 grams: dietary fiber;
- 2 grams: monounsaturated fat;
- 488 milligrams: sodium;
- 1 gram: polyunsaturated fat;
- 46 grams: carbohydrates;
- 4 grams: sugars;
- 13 grams: protein;

28. Ramen With Charred Scallions, Green Beans And Chile Oil

Serving: 4 servings | Prep: | Cook: |Ready in: 30mins

Ingredients

- For the Chile Oil:
- 2 tablespoons red-pepper flakes (see Tip)
- 1 ½ teaspoons kosher salt
- ½ cup neutral oil, such as grapeseed, vegetable or canola
- 1 (1-inch) piece ginger, peeled and finely chopped
- 2 garlic cloves, finely chopped
- 2 teaspoons toasted white sesame seeds
- 1 teaspoon sesame oil
- For the Noodles:

- Kosher salt
- 4 (3-ounce) packages ramen noodles, seasoning packs discarded
- 2 bunches scallions (10 to 12 scallions), white and green parts separated and cut into 2-inch pieces
- 2 to 3 tablespoons neutral oil, such as grapeseed, vegetable or canola
- 10 ounces green beans, trimmed and halved diagonally
- 1 (2-inch) piece ginger, peeled and julienned
- White pepper
- 1 tablespoon toasted white sesame seeds

Direction

- Prepare the chile oil: Add the red-pepper flakes and salt to a heatproof bowl. Place the oil, ginger and garlic in a small saucepan, and heat over medium until it bubbles, 2 to 3 minutes. Remove from the heat and very carefully pour the hot oil over the red-pepper flakes. Add the sesame seeds and sesame oil, and stir well. Set aside while you make the rest of the dish. (Chile oil can be stored in an airtight jar at room temperature for up to a month and indefinitely in the refrigerator.)
- Prepare the noodles: Bring a large pot of salted water to a boil. Add the ramen and cook according to package instructions, about 3 minutes, until the noodles are just tender. Drain, rinse with cold water and drain well again.
- Slice the white parts of your scallions lengthwise, in half or quarters, depending on thickness, to make cooking faster.
- Heat a wok or large (12-inch), deep skillet on high. When smoking hot, add 1 tablespoon of oil, toss in the green beans and season with salt. Cook, tossing the beans, for 2 to 3 minutes, until charred. Remove the beans from the wok, and set aside.
- Heat the same wok or skillet over high, and when smoking, add 1 to 2 tablespoons of oil, along with the scallions (white and green parts) and the ginger. Allow the scallions and ginger to sizzle for 20 to 30 seconds, to release

their aromas, then stir-fry for 2 to 3 minutes, until the scallions have a nice scorch.

- Add the green beans and noodles back to the pan, along with 2 or 3 tablespoons of the chile oil (reserve some for serving), and season with salt and pepper. Toss well to combine, just until the noodles are heated through. To serve, divide the noodles into bowls, top with toasted sesame seeds and more chile oil.

29. Rice Noodle Salad With Salted Peanuts And Herbs

Serving: 4 servings | Prep: | Cook: | Ready in: 25mins

Ingredients

- For the salad:
- 1 bunch radishes, thinly sliced
- 1 large carrot, grated
- 1 ½ tablespoons rice wine vinegar
- 2 teaspoons granulated sugar
- Pinch of fine sea salt
- 8 ounces pad Thai rice noodles
- For the dressing:
- 3 tablespoons lime juice (from about 2 limes), plus more to taste
- 2 tablespoons grapeseed or other neutral oil
- 1 ½ tablespoons fish sauce
- 1 (1-inch) piece fresh ginger, peeled and finely grated
- 1 garlic clove, finely grated or mashed to a paste
- 1 to 2 bird's-eye or serrano chiles, thinly sliced
- For the garnish:
- 1 cup thinly sliced cucumber, preferably Persian
- Handful of lettuce leaves, torn if large
- 2 scallions, thinly sliced
- Large handful of fresh, soft herbs, such as dill, mint and cilantro
- ½ cup roasted and salted peanuts, coarsely chopped
- 4 hard-boiled eggs (optional)

Direction

- In a medium bowl, toss radishes and carrot with vinegar, sugar and salt, and let sit while preparing remaining ingredients.
- Cook rice noodles according to package instructions. Immediately transfer to a colander and rinse under cold water to cool. Set aside to drain.
- In a small bowl, prepare the dressing: Stir together lime juice, oil, fish sauce, ginger, garlic and chiles.
- Pile noodles in a large bowl, then top with radish and carrot mixture and any juices from the bowl, cucumber, lettuce, scallions, herbs, peanuts and eggs, if using. Drizzle the dressing over the top.

30. Rice Noodles With Chile And Basil

Serving: 4 servings | Prep: | Cook: | Ready in: 40mins

Ingredients

- 12 ounces rice stick noodles
- 2 tablespoons peanut or vegetable oil
- 1 tablespoon minced garlic
- 1 teaspoon minced hot chilies, or crushed red pepper flakes, or to taste
- 1 teaspoon sugar
- Salt and freshly ground black pepper
- 2 tablespoons nam pla, or to taste
- 1 tablespoon lime juice, or to taste
- ½ cup roughly chopped Thai or other basil or mint

Direction

- Soak the rice noodles in hot water to cover for about 30 minutes. Meanwhile, bring a pot of water to a boil. When the noodles are soft, drain them and then immerse them in the boiling water for about 30 seconds. Drain and rinse.

- Heat the oil in a deep skillet (preferably nonstick) over medium-high heat. Add the garlic and chilies and cook about 30 seconds, stirring. Raise the heat to high, add the noodles and sugar and toss to coat. Season with salt and pepper.
- When the noodles are hot, add the nam pla and lime. Taste and adjust seasonings, then stir in the basil or mint and serve.

Nutrition Information

- 385: calories;
- 8 grams: fat;
- 2 grams: sugars;
- 6 grams: protein;
- 1 gram: polyunsaturated fat;
- 0 grams: trans fat;
- 5 grams: monounsaturated fat;
- 71 grams: carbohydrates;
- 876 milligrams: sodium;

31. Rice Noodles With Seared Pork, Carrots And Herbs

Serving: 4 to 6 servings | Prep: | Cook: |Ready in: 20mins

Ingredients

- ⅓ cup fish sauce
- ¼ cup dark, pure maple syrup
- 2 tablespoons grapeseed or other neutral oil
- Black pepper
- 2 large shallots, thinly sliced (3/4 cup)
- 1 long red finger chile, thinly sliced (1/3 cup)
- 3 small garlic cloves, minced (1 tablespoon)
- 4 thin (1/2-inch) boneless pork chops (3/4 to 1 pound total)
- ⅓ cup fresh lime juice (from about 3 limes), plus lime wedges for serving
- 3 carrots, peeled and julienned (2 cups)
- Kosher salt
- 8 to 9 ounces thin rice vermicelli noodles

- 2 packed cups torn fresh herbs, such as cilantro, basil and dill (2 1/2 ounces), plus more for garnish

Direction

- Whisk the fish sauce, syrup, 1 tablespoon oil, and 1/2 teaspoon pepper in a large bowl. Stir in the shallots, chile and garlic. Transfer 2 tablespoons liquid to a large shallow dish and add the pork. Turn to evenly coat and let stand until ready to cook.
- Stir the lime juice into the sauce in the bowl. Add the carrots and toss until evenly coated. Let stand.
- Bring a large saucepan of water to a boil. Meanwhile, heat a large skillet over medium-high heat. Season the pork with salt and pepper. Heat the remaining tablespoon oil in the skillet and swirl to coat the bottom. Add the pork and cook, turning once, until seared and just rosy in the center, 2 to 4 minutes per side. Transfer to a plate and let stand.
- Put the noodles in the boiling water, stir well, and remove from the heat. Let stand until softened, 3 to 5 minutes. Drain very well, then transfer to the sauce in the bowl. Toss until evenly coated.
- Cut the pork into thin slices and add to the noodles with any accumulated juices. Toss well. Toss in the herbs until well mixed. The mixture may look a bit soupy. As it sits and cools, the noodles will absorb the liquid. Serve hot, warm, or at room temperature with more herbs and lime wedges.

Nutrition Information

- 452: calories;
- 5 grams: monounsaturated fat;
- 50 grams: carbohydrates;
- 12 grams: sugars;
- 3 grams: dietary fiber;
- 29 grams: protein;
- 1413 milligrams: sodium;
- 15 grams: fat;
- 2 grams: polyunsaturated fat;

- 0 grams: trans fat;

32. Savory Thai Noodles With Seared Brussels Sprouts

Serving: 3 to 4 servings | Prep: | Cook: | Ready in: 30mins

Ingredients

- For the sauce:
- ⅓ cup tamari sauce
- ⅓ cup packed brown sugar
- 3 tablespoons white miso
- 3 tablespoons tomato paste
- 2 tablespoons tamarind concentrate
- 1 teaspoon red-pepper flakes
- For the noodles:
- 8 ounces Thai rice noodles
- 3 tablespoons plus 1 teaspoon coconut oil
- 1 bunch (6 to 8) scallions, trimmed
- Kosher salt
- 8 ounces trimmed brussels sprouts, shredded or quartered
- 4 cloves garlic, minced
- 2 cups loosely packed cilantro leaves and thin stems
- 4 ounces mung bean sprouts (optional)
- ½ cup salted roasted peanuts, lightly cracked in a mortar or coarsely chopped
- 1 red chile, such as Fresno, thinly sliced (optional)
- 4 lime wedges, for serving

Direction

- Make the sauce: In a blender or bowl, combine all the ingredients and mix until smooth. It should be thick but pourable like barbecue sauce; add water as needed to thin it out.
- Cook noodles for stir-frying according to the package directions; they should be slightly underdone. After draining, rinse well with cold water to stop the cooking. Toss noodles in 1 teaspoon coconut oil to prevent sticking.
- Cut scallions: Thinly slice the white parts, and cut the pale and dark green parts into 1-inch lengths.
- Heat a wok or large nonstick skillet over high. Add 2 tablespoons coconut oil and sprinkle in salt. Add brussels sprouts and sear, tossing occasionally, until browned and cooked through, about 5 minutes. Remove from the pan and set aside.
- In the same pan over high heat, heat remaining 1 tablespoon coconut oil. Add scallions and cook, stirring often, just until wilted, about 2 minutes. Add garlic, stir, then pour in about half the sauce and stir until bubbling.
- Add noodles and cook, tossing in the sauce until cooked through, about 2 minutes. Add the remaining sauce, cooked brussels sprouts, cilantro and bean sprouts, if using; toss to coat and heat through.
- Divide among plates. Garnish with peanuts, chile and lime wedges (if using) and serve immediately.

33. Shanghai Stir Fried Chunky Noodles

Serving: 3 to 4 servings | Prep: | Cook: | Ready in: 35mins

Ingredients

- 6 ounces lean pork, from a boneless pork loin chop or a tenderloin
- ½ teaspoon plus 2 tablespoons light soy sauce
- 1 ½ teaspoons Shaoxing wine
- 1 teaspoon cornstarch
- 1 pound fresh Shanghai noodles or Japanese udon noodles
- 2 tablespoons peanut or vegetable oil, plus a splash
- 1 tablespoon dark soy sauce
- 2 tablespoons chicken stock

- 10 ounces green baby bok choy or 2 large handfuls of baby spinach
- Salt and ground white pepper

Direction

- Cut the pork evenly into 1/4-inch slices, then into 1/8-inch slivers.
- In a small bowl, combine 1/2 teaspoon light soy sauce, the Shaoxing wine, the cornstarch and 1 tablespoon cold water and mix well. Add pork and marinate until ready to cook.
- Bring a large, deep pot of water to a boil. Add noodles and cook for 2 minutes. Turn the cooked noodles into a colander and rinse with cold water. Shake them dry and toss with a splash of oil, stirring thoroughly to prevent sticking.
- In a small bowl, combine remaining light soy sauce, the dark soy sauce and the chicken stock and set aside. Heat 1 tablespoon oil in a large, seasoned wok over high heat until oil just begins to smoke. Add pork, leaving the marinade behind, and stir-fry swiftly to separate. When they are just cooked, remove from wok and set aside.
- Clean and re-season the wok, if necessary, then return it to high heat with the remaining oil. Add noodles and soy sauce mixture and stir-fry until piping hot. Add bok choy or spinach and continue to stir-fry briefly until wilted. Stir in the pork and season to taste with salt and white pepper. Serve.

Nutrition Information

- 574: calories;
- 3 grams: polyunsaturated fat;
- 89 grams: carbohydrates;
- 4 grams: sugars;
- 26 grams: protein;
- 12 grams: fat;
- 7 grams: monounsaturated fat;
- 5 grams: dietary fiber;
- 594 milligrams: sodium;
- 2 grams: saturated fat;
- 0 grams: trans fat;

34. Slow Cooker Chicken Ramen With Bok Choy And Miso

Serving: 4 to 5 servings | Prep: | Cook: | Ready in: 6hours20mins

Ingredients

- 3 to 3 ½ pounds skin-on whole chicken legs (about 5 legs)
- ½ heaping cup sweet white or yellow miso, plus more to taste
- 2 scallions, trimmed and halved, plus more for topping
- 3 garlic cloves, smashed
- 4 dried shiitake mushrooms (optional)
- 1 (5-by-3-inch) piece dried kombu (optional)
- 1 pound baby bok choy, cored and roughly chopped
- 2 tablespoons tamari, plus more to taste
- 2 tablespoons mirin, plus more to taste
- 12 to 16 ounces ramen, cooked and drained
- Soft boiled eggs, sesame seeds and toasted nori sheets, for topping

Direction

- Put the chicken legs in a 5- to 8-quart slow cooker, and crumble the miso on top. Add the scallions, garlic cloves, shiitake mushrooms (if using) and 6 cups water. Stir well to combine. Cook until the chicken is tender, at least 4 hours and up to 6 hours on low. If it's more convenient, you can let the slow cooker switch to warm after 6 hours. The soup will hold on warm for about another 2 hours before the chicken begins to dry out.
- Switch the heat to high. With a slotted spoon, remove the chicken, scallions, garlic and shiitakes, and place in a bowl. Set aside to cool. Stir in kombu, bok choy, tamari and mirin. Cover and let cook until the bok choy is wilted and tender, 5 to 10 minutes. Remove and discard the kombu. Coarsely shred

chicken meat into the soup, discarding the skin, bone, scallions, garlic and shiitakes. Taste the soup and whisk in a few more spoonfuls of miso or tamari, if desired.

- Divide the noodles among 4 or 5 bowls, and ladle the soup on top. Top each with sliced scallion, a halved soft boiled egg, sesame seeds and a piece of nori.

Nutrition Information

- 1171: calories;
- 22 grams: saturated fat;
- 3198 milligrams: sodium;
- 71 grams: fat;
- 0 grams: trans fat;
- 28 grams: monounsaturated fat;
- 14 grams: polyunsaturated fat;
- 60 grams: carbohydrates;
- 5 grams: sugars;
- 70 grams: protein;

35. Soba Noodle And Steak Salad With Ginger Lime Dressing

Serving: 4 servings | Prep: | Cook: | Ready in: 30mins

Ingredients

- 8 ounces soba noodles
- ¼ cup soy sauce
- ¼ cup lime juice (from 2 limes)
- 2 teaspoons finely grated fresh ginger
- 1 teaspoon sesame oil
- ½ teaspoon light brown sugar
- 1 pound hanger or skirt steak, at room temperature
- Kosher salt and black pepper
- 1 tablespoon canola or grapeseed oil, plus more as needed
- 8 ounces baby bok choy, halved lengthwise if large
- 1 cup julienned or thinly sliced carrots
- 3 to 4 radishes, thinly sliced (optional)

- ½ cup thinly sliced scallions (2 or 3 scallions)
- ¼ cup fresh mint, torn
- Flaky salt, for serving (optional)

Direction

- Cook soba noodles according to package instructions. Rinse under cold water, drain well and set aside. Meanwhile, in a medium bowl, whisk together the soy sauce, lime juice, ginger, sesame oil and brown sugar; set aside.
- Season the steak well with salt and pepper. Heat a large cast-iron pan over medium-high until very hot, 2 to 3 minutes. Add the canola oil and when it shimmers, add the steak and cook, undisturbed, until it begins to get crisp and golden on the outside, 3 to 4 minutes. (If you are using skirt steak, you may need to cut it into 2 or 3 pieces to fit in the pan, then cook for 2 to 3 minutes.) Flip and finish cooking, about 3 minutes more for medium-rare. Set aside and allow the steak to rest while you prepare the rest of the salad.
- Turn heat to medium and add the bok choy. Season with salt and pepper and cook, stirring frequently, until it begins to brown and char in spots, 2 to 3 minutes, adding another teaspoon or so of oil if needed to help if the pan is too dry. Remove from the heat.
- In a large bowl, toss the soba noodles, carrots, radishes (if using) and half the scallions. Drizzle with the ginger-lime dressing to taste and divide among plates or in serving bowls. Thinly slice the steaks against the grain and top each portion with some of the steak and the bok choy. Scatter the remaining scallions and the mint over top and season with flaky salt, if desired. Serve with any leftover dressing in a small bowl to be passed at the table.

36. Soba Noodles With Chicken And Snap Peas

Serving: 4 servings | Prep: | Cook: | Ready in: 20mins

Ingredients

- 3 tablespoons rice vinegar
- 3 tablespoons honey
- Kosher salt
- 1 cup very thinly sliced peeled daikon radish
- 8 ounces sugar snap peas, strings removed (3 cups)
- 2 bundles soba noodles (8 to 9 ounces)
- 3 tablespoons soy sauce
- 2 tablespoons sesame oil
- ½ teaspoon red-pepper flakes, plus more for serving
- 3 cups shredded cooked chicken
- Sliced scallions and toasted sesame seeds, for serving

Direction

- Bring a large saucepan of water to a boil. Meanwhile, mix the vinegar, 1 tablespoon honey and 1 teaspoon salt in a small bowl. Add the daikon and press into the mixture to submerge as much as possible. Let stand until ready to serve, mixing occasionally.
- Add 1/4 cup salt to the boiling water. Add the snap peas and cook just until bright green and tender, about 30 seconds to 1 minute. Using a spider or slotted spoon, transfer to a colander and immediately rinse under cold water until cool. Drain well.
- Add the noodles to the boiling water. Cook, stirring occasionally, until just tender, 4 to 8 minutes. Drain, rinse under cold water until cool and drain again.
- While the noodles cook, whisk the soy sauce, sesame oil, red-pepper flakes and remaining 2 tablespoons honey in a large bowl. Add the chicken, soba and snap peas and toss until evenly coated. Season to taste with salt.
- Divide among bowls. Drain the daikon pickles and arrange on top, then garnish with the scallions, sesame seeds and additional red-pepper flakes.

Nutrition Information

- 559: calories;
- 761 milligrams: sodium;
- 17 grams: fat;
- 4 grams: saturated fat;
- 0 grams: trans fat;
- 5 grams: dietary fiber;
- 6 grams: monounsaturated fat;
- 63 grams: carbohydrates;
- 18 grams: sugars;
- 38 grams: protein;

37. Southern Macaroni And Cheese

Serving: 8 to 10 servings | Prep: | Cook: | Ready in: 45mins

Ingredients

- Kosher salt and black pepper
- 1 pound elbow macaroni
- 2 cups whole milk
- 2 large eggs
- 4 cups shredded extra-sharp Cheddar (about 16 ounces)
- ½ cup unsalted butter (1 stick), melted
- 2 cups shredded Colby Jack (about 8 ounces)

Direction

- Heat oven to 350 degrees. Bring a large pot of generously salted water to a boil. Add macaroni and cook according to package directions until a little under al dente, about 4 minutes. Transfer to a colander and rinse under cold water to stop cooking. Set aside.
- In a large bowl, whisk milk and eggs. Add cooked macaroni, 2 cups extra-sharp Cheddar, melted butter, 1 1/2 teaspoons salt and 1/2 teaspoon pepper, and stir until well combined.

- Add half the macaroni mixture to a 9-by-13-inch baking dish in an even layer. Sprinkle 1 1/2 cups Colby Jack evenly on top. Spread the remaining macaroni mixture on top in an even layer. Cover with aluminum foil, transfer to the middle rack of the oven and bake for 30 minutes.
- Remove from oven. Carefully remove and discard the aluminum foil. Top the macaroni mixture with the remaining 2 cups Cheddar and 1/2 cup Colby Jack. Broil on top rack until cheese is browned in spots, 3 to 5 minutes. (The broiled cheese can go from golden to burnt fairly quickly, so keep a close eye on it.)
- Remove from oven and let cool until the macaroni and cheese is fully set, 10 to 15 minutes. (The mixture may first appear jiggly, but it will firm up as it cools.) Serve warm.

38. Spicy Glass Noodles With Shiitake Mushrooms And Cabbage

Serving: 4 servings | Prep: | Cook: | Ready in: 45mins

Ingredients

- 4 bundles dried glass noodles (about 5 ounces)
- 8 dried shiitake mushrooms (about 1/2 ounce)
- 3 tablespoons grapeseed oil
- 2 garlic cloves, peeled and minced
- 1 (2-inch) piece fresh ginger, peeled and julienned
- 1 scallion, trimmed and finely chopped
- 1 pound Napa or green cabbage (about 1/3 medium cabbage), cored and thinly sliced into 1/4-inch-wide strips
- 1 teaspoon Indian or Vietnamese curry powder
- 4 tablespoons soy sauce
- 1 tablespoon toasted sesame oil
- 3 tablespoons fresh cilantro leaves and stems

Direction

- Place the noodles in a large bowl, cover with room-temperature water and soak until pliable, about 30 minutes. Drain. Place dried shiitakes in a medium bowl, cover with room-temperature water and soak until hydrated and soft, about 30 minutes. Drain the mushrooms, remove their stems, and julienne the caps.
- While the noodles and mushrooms soak, heat the grapeseed oil in a large lidded skillet over medium-high, uncovered. Stir-fry the garlic, ginger and scallion until light golden, about 1 minute. Add the shiitakes and continue to stir-fry until golden, about 2 minutes.
- Stir in the cabbage and curry powder, then 3 tablespoons soy sauce. Reduce heat to medium, cover and cook until the cabbage is wilted and has given up its natural juices, 5 to 7 minutes.
- Add the drained noodles and remaining 1 tablespoon soy sauce. Increase heat to high, and stir-fry until noodles absorb the juices and are cooked through yet still chewy, 1 to 2 minutes. Drizzle with sesame oil, toss well, sprinkle with cilantro and serve immediately.

39. Spicy Minced Shrimp With Rice Noodles

Serving: 4 servings | Prep: | Cook: | Ready in: 45mins

Ingredients

- 1 pound dry flat rice noodles (sometimes called rice stick noodles)
- About 1 pound wild shrimp, in the shell, fresh, or frozen and thawed (about 24 pieces)
- 2 fresh red Fresno chiles or green Serrano chiles, seeds removed, if desired, finely chopped (or substitute 1 teaspoon red-pepper flakes)
- 2 tablespoon dried shrimp, finely chopped (optional)
- 1 tablespoon rice vinegar

- 2 tablespoons soy sauce
- 2 teaspoons toasted sesame oil, plus 1 teaspoon for drizzling
- 2 tablespoons mirin or sherry (if using sherry add 1 teaspoon sugar)
- 1 teaspoon grated garlic (about 2 or 3 cloves)
- 1 tablespoon grated ginger
- 1 teaspoon kosher salt, plus more as necessary
- 3 tablespoons chopped scallions
- 3 tablespoons coconut or vegetable oil
- Basil leaves, cilantro sprigs and 2 tablespoons chopped roasted peanuts, for garnish
- Lime wedges, for serving (optional)

Direction

- Soak noodles in a large bowl of lukewarm water. Leave until softened but still firm, about 15 minutes. Drain and rinse well with cold water. Set aside. (Alternately, boil noodles for 2 or 3 minutes, then drain and rinse well with cold water.)
- Meanwhile, peel shrimp and make the seasoned shrimp mixture: With a large knife, cut the shrimp crosswise into rough 1/4- to 1/2-inch slices. In a large bowl, combine shrimp, chopped chiles, dried shrimp (if using), rice vinegar, soy sauce, 2 teaspoons sesame oil, mirin, garlic, ginger, salt and scallions. Mix well to distribute ingredients throughout. Refrigerate for at least 20 minutes (or, preferably, up to 24 hours).
- Put coconut oil in a large wok or wide cast-iron skillet over high heat. When oil looks wavy, add shrimp-sausage mixture, breaking it up with a wooden spoon, until it looks crumbly. Stir-fry until pieces are lightly browned, about 3 or 4 minutes.
- Add noodles to pan and toss briefly, just to heat through. Drizzle with 1 teaspoon sesame oil. Taste and add a little more salt if necessary. Transfer to bowls and garnish with basil leaves, cilantro sprigs, chopped peanuts and lime wedges, if using.

Nutrition Information

- 607: calories;
- 1289 milligrams: sodium;
- 12 grams: fat;
- 1 gram: saturated fat;
- 94 grams: carbohydrates;
- 2 grams: dietary fiber;
- 23 grams: protein;
- 0 grams: sugars;
- 8 grams: monounsaturated fat;

40. Spicy Pan Fried Noodles

Serving: 2 servings | Prep: | Cook: | Ready in: 20mins

Ingredients

- 1 cup thinly sliced scallions (about a bunch; use both whites and greens)
- 3 tablespoons soy sauce, more to taste
- 1 tablespoon grated fresh ginger
- 2 teaspoons rice wine or sherry vinegar
- 1 teaspoon sesame oil
- ¼ teaspoon kosher salt, more as needed
- 6 ounces Chinese (also called Hong Kong) egg noodles, soba noodles or rice noodles
- 2 ½ tablespoons peanut, grapeseed, safflower or vegetable oil, more as needed
- 5 garlic cloves, thinly sliced
- 2 large eggs, beaten with a fork
- 2 cups washed baby spinach or 1/2 cup thawed edamame (optional)
- 1 to 2 teaspoons sriracha or other hot sauce, or to taste
- Juice of 1/2 lime, or to taste
- 1 cup cilantro leaves
- 2 tablespoons sesame seeds or chopped roasted peanuts, optional

Direction

- In a small bowl, combine the scallions, soy sauce, ginger, rice wine or vinegar, sesame oil and salt. Let stand while you prepare the noodles.

- In a large pot of boiling water, cook noodles until they are halfway done according to package instructions. (They should still be quite firm.) Drain well and toss with 1/2 tablespoon of the peanut oil to keep them from sticking, and spread them out on a plate or baking sheet.
- In a large skillet over medium-high heat, warm the remaining 2 tablespoons of peanut oil. Add the garlic and cook until crisp and golden around the edges, 1 to 2 minutes. Add half the scallion mixture and stir-fry until fragrant, about 1 minute. Add noodles; stir-fry until noodles are hot and lightly coated with sauce, about 30 seconds. Add eggs, spinach or edamame if using, sriracha, and remaining scallion mixture and continue to stir-fry until the eggs are cooked, 1 to 2 minutes longer. Remove from heat and stir in lime juice. Garnish with cilantro and sesame seeds or peanuts.

Nutrition Information

- 629: calories;
- 5 grams: dietary fiber;
- 1514 milligrams: sodium;
- 4 grams: sugars;
- 6 grams: polyunsaturated fat;
- 71 grams: carbohydrates;
- 29 grams: fat;
- 0 grams: trans fat;
- 16 grams: monounsaturated fat;
- 22 grams: protein;

41. Spicy Sesame Noodles With Chicken And Peanuts

Serving: 4 servings | Prep: | Cook: | Ready in: 30mins

Ingredients

- 1 ½ tablespoons red-pepper flakes
- 1 ½ tablespoons low-sodium soy sauce
- 1 ½ teaspoons toasted sesame oil, plus more as needed
- Kosher salt and black pepper
- ½ cup plus 1 tablespoon neutral oil, like grapeseed or vegetable
- 6 tablespoons roasted, salted peanuts, coarsely chopped
- Rind of 1/2 orange, peeled into 2- to 3-inch strips
- 1 pound ground chicken
- 10 to 12 ounces ramen or udon noodles, preferably fresh
- 3 tablespoons finely chopped chives

Direction

- In a medium heatproof bowl, stir together the red-pepper flakes, soy sauce and sesame oil. Set next to the stovetop.
- Bring a large pot of salted water to boil. Meanwhile, in a large (12-inch) skillet over medium heat, cook the 1/2 cup oil, peanuts and orange rind, shaking the pan occasionally, until the peanuts are golden and bubbling, 3 to 5 minutes. Immediately pour the contents of the skillet over the red-pepper mixture (be careful of splattering!) and set aside. (Once cool, the chile oil will keep in the refrigerator for 2 weeks in an airtight container.)
- Meanwhile, in the same skillet, heat the remaining tablespoon oil over medium-high. Add the chicken and press it down with a wooden spoon into a thin layer. Season with salt and a generous amount of black pepper and cook, without stirring, occasionally pressing the layer of chicken down, until the bottom is browned, 5 to 7 minutes. Break the chicken up into small pieces and cook, stirring occasionally, until cooked through, 1 to 2 minutes more.
- While the chicken cooks, cook the noodles according to package directions, until chewy but not soft. Drain and toss with a bit of sesame oil.
- Remove and discard the orange rind from the chile oil. Off the heat, add the chile oil to the chicken and stir to coat, scraping up any

browned bits from the pan. Add the noodles and toss to coat. Top with chives and serve at once.

42. Spring Ramen Bowl With Snap Peas And Asparagus

Serving: 4 servings | Prep: | Cook: | Ready in: 1hours30mins

Ingredients

- For the ramen:
- 8 ounces asparagus, preferably thick stalks
- 4 dried shiitake mushrooms
- 2 plump garlic cloves, smashed
- 4 2-inch squares kombu, or 2 longer sticks
- 2 tablespoons white or yellow miso paste
- 1 teaspoon fine sea salt, more to taste
- 4 ounces sugar snap peas
- 8 ounces dried or 12 ounces fresh ramen noodles
- 2 2-inch squares toasted nori
- 4 large hard-boiled eggs, semi-firm or firm yolks (optional)
- Zest of 1/2 to 1 lemon, to taste
- Freshly grated ginger, to taste
- Toasted sesame oil, for garnish
- For the frizzled scallion garnish (optional):
- Neutral oil, such as canola or grapeseed
- ½ bunch scallions, trimmed and cut into 3-inch matchsticks
- Fine sea salt

Direction

- Snap off the tough ends of the asparagus and set the top parts aside. Combine the tough asparagus ends, mushrooms, garlic and 9 cups water in a stockpot or saucepan and bring to a boil. Reduce heat and simmer for 20 minutes. Add kombu, remove from the heat, and let stand for 30 minutes. Strain out and discard the solids and return the broth to the stockpot.
- While the broth is simmering, prepare the frizzled scallions, if using: Heat 1/2 inch of oil in a small skillet or saucepan over medium heat. Test temperature by adding a piece of scallion; it should sizzle on contact. Add scallions and cook, stirring frequently, until brown all over but not burned. Use a spider or slotted spoon to transfer to a paper-towel-lined plate. Sprinkle with salt and allow to cool. (Use within a few hours.)
- In a tall glass or measuring cup, combine miso and a ladleful of hot broth. Purée thoroughly with an immersion blender until smooth. (Alternately, carefully purée in a blender.) Pour mixture back into the stockpot and bring to a bare simmer. Add salt and taste, adding more if necessary. Keep covered over low heat until ready to serve.
- Use a vegetable peeler to shave the asparagus spears into ribbons. (It's easiest to do this by laying them flat on a cutting board, and using a Y peeler.)
- Bring another saucepan of salted water to boil and prepare an ice bath. Remove the fibrous strings from the snap peas. (To do so, pinch one end and pull along the straight edge of the pea as if it's a zipper.) Once the water comes to a boil, add snap peas and blanch for 90 seconds. Use a slotted spoon to transfer peas to the ice bath. Reserve the boiling water.
- Add noodles to the boiling water, in a strainer or the pasta insert that comes with a stockpot, and cook until tender, usually 4 to 7 minutes for dried or 60 to 90 seconds for fresh. Lift out the noodles, reserving the cooking water, and rinse the noodles thoroughly under cold running water. Quickly dunk them back into the hot water to reheat. Divide among four bowls.
- Just before serving, wave the nori squares over the flame of a gas burner a few times, until the corners curl and they turn crisp, or roast under a broiler, flipping periodically. Slice into thin strips with a chef's knife or crumble with your fingers.
- Arrange asparagus, snap peas and egg halves, if using, over the noodles in each bowl. Add a

pinch of lemon zest and a few gratings of ginger to each bowl, then cover with the piping hot broth. Divide frizzled scallions on top, if using, then garnish each serving with a few drops of sesame oil and the nori. Serve immediately.

Nutrition Information

- 344: calories;
- 48 grams: carbohydrates;
- 10 grams: protein;
- 1410 milligrams: sodium;
- 14 grams: fat;
- 5 grams: sugars;
- 0 grams: trans fat;
- 2 grams: polyunsaturated fat;

43. Sweet And Spicy Tofu With Soba Noodles

Serving: 4 servings | Prep: | Cook: | Ready in: 30mins

Ingredients

- 1 ½ (14-ounce) packages firm tofu, drained
- 2 tablespoons canola oil
- 2 tablespoons sesame oil
- 1 (8-ounce) package all-buckwheat soba noodles
- 4 garlic cloves, smashed
- 1 (1-inch) piece ginger, peeled and thinly sliced
- 1 small bunch green onions, white and green parts separated, cut into 2-inch matchsticks
- ⅓ cup soy sauce or tamari
- 3 tablespoons dark brown sugar
- 1 teaspoon black pepper
- Pinch of red-pepper flakes
- 4 mini or 1 large, thin-skinned cucumber, thinly sliced
- 4 radishes, thinly sliced
- Handful of cilantro leaves, for serving
- 1 lime, cut in wedges, for serving

Direction

- Drain the tofu in a colander, or dry on paper-towel lined plate while you prep the remaining ingredients, about 10 minutes. Meanwhile, bring a small pot of water to a boil for the soba noodles.
- Cut tofu into 1-inch cubes. Heat a cast-iron skillet over medium-high heat. Add the vegetable oil and 1 tablespoon of the sesame oil. When the oil shimmers, add the tofu in a single layer, in batches if needed and cook until golden on all sides, turning as needed when the tofu releases easily from the pan, about 8 to 10 minutes total. Lift the tofu out of the pan with a spatula and transfer to a new paper-towel-lined plate.
- Meanwhile, cook the soba in boiling water for 5 to 8 minutes (or according to package directions), until just al dente, stirring frequently. Drain and rinse in cold water until the noodles no longer feel sticky.
- Add garlic, ginger and whites of the onions to the skillet, along with the remaining tablespoon sesame oil, reduce the heat to medium, and cook until the oil is fragrant, stirring constantly, about 1 minute.
- Add cooked and drained soba noodles to the pan, along with soy sauce, sugar, black pepper, red pepper and reserved green onions; toss together until the noodles are coated. Gently toss in the tofu until all the pieces are covered in the sauce.
- Remove from the heat, and sprinkle cucumber, radish and cilantro on top. Serve warm or at room temperature, with lime.

Nutrition Information

- 607: calories;
- 5 grams: dietary fiber;
- 35 grams: protein;
- 1652 milligrams: sodium;
- 4 grams: saturated fat;
- 12 grams: polyunsaturated fat;
- 66 grams: carbohydrates;

- 28 grams: fat;
- 0 grams: trans fat;
- 10 grams: monounsaturated fat;
- 9 grams: sugars;

44. Tangy Pork Noodle Salad With Lime And Lots Of Herbs

Serving: 4 servings | Prep: | Cook: | Ready in: 40mins

Ingredients

- 1 teaspoon finely grated lime zest
- 2 ½ tablespoons fresh lime juice, plus more to taste
- 2 tablespoons fresh orange juice
- 2 tablespoons fish sauce, plus more as needed
- 1 tablespoon honey
- Fine sea salt
- 4 tablespoons grapeseed or safflower oil
- ½ cup thinly sliced shallot (1 large)
- 6 ounces pad Thai or other flat rice noodles
- 2 garlic cloves, finely grated or mashed to a paste
- 1 (2-inch) piece ginger, peeled and grated (about 2 teaspoons)
- 1 Thai or serrano chile, thinly sliced and seeded if you like
- 1 pound ground pork (or turkey)
- 1 cup thinly sliced cucumbers
- 2 scallions, white and green parts, sliced
- 1 ¼ cups cherry tomatoes, halved
- 1 cup mung or other bean sprouts (or 1 cup lettuce)
- 1 packed cup mint leaves
- 1 packed cup cilantro or basil sprigs, or a combination
- 2 cups shredded romaine or other crisp lettuce
- Red-pepper flakes, for serving
- Lime wedges, for serving

Direction

- In a small bowl, whisk together lime zest and juice, orange juice, 2 tablespoons fish sauce, honey and a small pinch of salt. Pour half of the mixture into a large bowl and whisk in 3 tablespoons grapeseed oil and the shallots. Set both mixtures aside.
- Cook noodles in salted water and according to package directions. Rinse under running water to remove any excess starch, then drain well and add to bowl with shallots, tossing well. Set aside while preparing remaining ingredients.
- Heat remaining 1 tablespoon grapeseed oil in a large skillet over medium-high heat. Add garlic, ginger and chile, and cook until lightly golden and aromatic, about 1 minute. Add pork and stir, breaking up pieces with a wooden spoon. Cook without stirring too often, until browned, about 8 minutes. Pour in lime juice mixture from the small bowl. Simmer gently until most of the liquid is evaporated, stirring to coat pork in the glaze, another 1 minute. Remove from heat and set aside to cool slightly.
- Add pork, cucumbers, scallions, cherry tomatoes, bean sprouts and herbs to the noodles and toss well to combine. Taste and add more fish sauce, lime juice or both. Just before serving, toss in lettuce, and serve sprinkled with red-pepper flakes with lime wedges on the side.

45. Thai Red Curry Noodles With Vegetables

Serving: 4 servings | Prep: | Cook: | Ready in: 50mins

Ingredients

- For the paste:
- ¼ cup lightly packed cilantro leaves and stems (white roots, too, if available)
- 2 cloves garlic, roughly chopped
- 1 shallot, sliced

- 1 fresh hot red chile, seeded and roughly chopped
- 2 tablespoons prepared Thai red curry paste
- 1 tablespoon coconut oil
- 1 tablespoon grated fresh ginger
- 1 lemongrass stalk, tough outer leaves trimmed off, inner leaves finely chopped
- Finely grated zest and juice of 1 lime
- 2 teaspoons Asian fish sauce
- 1 teaspoon curry powder
- ¾ teaspoon cumin seeds
- ½ teaspoon ground coriander
- For the noodles:
- 3 tablespoons coconut oil
- 5 ounces sliced shiitake mushrooms (about 3 cups)
- 6 scallions, thinly sliced
- 3 cloves garlic, thinly sliced
- 1 fresh hot red chile, seeded and thinly sliced
- Kosher salt
- 4 ounces thin dried noodles, such as ramen, egg noodles, rice noodles, etc.
- 1 (14-ounce) can full-fat coconut milk
- 1 ½ tablespoons Asian fish sauce, more to taste
- Juice of 1/2 lime, plus more to taste
- 1 cup sliced red bell pepper
- 1 cup sliced snow peas or green beans
- 5 ounces baby bok choy, spinach or tatsoi torn into bite-size pieces
- Lime wedges, for garnish
- Optional garnishes (use all or any combination of the following): 1/2 cup thinly sliced radishes; torn basil, mint, or cilantro leaves; sesame seeds; halved hard-cooked eggs

Direction

- Prepare the curry paste: In a blender or mini food processor, combine cilantro, garlic, shallot, chile, red curry, coconut oil, ginger, lemongrass, zest and juice of 1 lime, fish sauce, curry powder, cumin and coriander. Blend into a paste, scraping down the sides of the blender as needed. If mixture is too thick to blend, add teaspoon or two of water as needed.

- In a large skillet, heat coconut oil over medium heat. Stir in mushrooms, half the scallions, garlic, chile and a large pinch of salt. Sauté until golden, 10 to 12 minutes.
- Meanwhile, cook the noodles according to package directions. Drain and set aside.
- Stir 1/4 cup curry paste mixture into skillet and cook until fragrant and darkened, 1 to 2 minutes. Stir coconut milk into skillet along with remaining 1 1/2 tablespoons fish sauce, and juice of 1/2 lime.
- Add red pepper, snow peas and 1/2 teaspoon salt. Cover and cook, stirring occasionally, until vegetables are softened, 3 to 5 minutes. Stir in bok choy and cook until wilted, 2 to 4 minutes longer.
- Fold in noodles, tossing until coated with sauce and heated through. Add fish sauce or lime juice to taste, and pass lime wedges at the table. Top with remaining scallions and any of the optional garnishes. Serve with lime wedges on the side. Store the extra curry paste in the refrigerator for up to 3 weeks, or freeze for up to 3 months.

46. The Big Lasagna

Serving: One 9-by-13-inch lasagna (8 to 12 servings) | Prep: | Cook: | Ready in: 2hours30mins

Ingredients

- For the Ricotta Filling:
- 4 tablespoons extra-virgin olive oil (if using fresh spinach)
- 1 pound fresh mature spinach, washed and ends trimmed, 1 pound baby spinach, or 1 1/2 cups frozen spinach, thawed
- Fine sea salt
- 2 pounds whole-milk or part-skim ricotta (about 4 cups)
- 6 ounces grated whole-milk or part-skim mozzarella, provolone or even string cheese (2 cups)

- 3 ounces freshly grated Parmesan, Asiago or Grana Padano (1 heaping cup)
- 20 large fresh basil leaves (from 1 bunch), finely chopped (about 3/4 cup), 2 tablespoons finely chopped fresh Italian parsley or chives, 1 teaspoon finely chopped fresh thyme or marjoram or 1 teaspoon dried Italian seasoning
- For the Béchamel:
- ½ cup unsalted butter (1 stick)
- ½ cup all-purpose flour
- 4 cups whole milk
- Fine sea salt
- Freshly ground black pepper
- Ground nutmeg (optional)
- For the Assembled Lasagna:
- 4 ½ cups Simple Tomato Sauce or 32 ounces store-bought marinara sauce (preferably without added sugar)
- Fine sea salt
- 1 recipe Homemade Lasagna Sheets, 16 fresh store-bought lasagna sheets, 2 (9-ounce) packages dried lasagna noodles (preferably without curly edges) or no-boil noodles (boiled until al dente)
- 1 ½ ounces grated Parmesan, Asiago or Grana Padano (1/2 cup)
- 3 ounces grated whole-milk or part-skim mozzarella, provolone or even string cheese (1 cup)

Direction

- Prepare the ricotta filling: If using fresh spinach, set a large skillet over high heat. (If using thawed frozen spinach, skip to Step 2.) When hot, add 2 tablespoons oil and half the fresh spinach. Season with a pinch of salt and sauté to wilt. Cook until stems are tender, about 3 minutes. Transfer to a baking sheet and allow to cool in a single layer. Repeat with remaining spinach.
- While spinach cools, combine ricotta, mozzarella, Parmesan, basil and a generous pinch of salt in a large bowl.
- Taking handfuls of the cooled or thawed spinach, squeeze out as much water as

possible, then chop finely and add to cheese mixture. Mix thoroughly, then taste and adjust seasoning for salt. (Filling makes about 6 cups.) Cover and set aside until ready to assemble lasagna. (Ricotta filling can be made 1 day in advance and refrigerated. Bring to room temperature before assembling lasagna.)

- Prepare the béchamel: Set a large, heavy-bottomed pot or Dutch oven over medium heat and add butter. Once butter has melted, whisk in flour, reduce heat to very low and cook for about 15 minutes, stirring regularly to prevent browning. After the mixture foams a bit, it will visibly transform — the butter will separate, the bubbles will reduce in size, and the mixture will look like freshly wet fine sand. Whisking vigorously, slowly pour in milk. Increase heat to medium and whisk until the mixture thickens, about 2 minutes. Add salt, pepper and nutmeg (if using) to taste.
- Return heat to low. Continue cooking, whisking regularly, for 10 to 15 minutes until the sauce is thick and smooth, with no raw flour flavor. Taste and adjust seasoning with salt. If béchamel is lumpy, strain through a fine sieve or purée with an immersion blender. (You'll have about 3 1/2 cups.) Press a piece of parchment or plastic against the surface of the sauce to prevent a skin from forming and set aside until ready to assemble lasagna. (Béchamel can be made up to 1 day in advance, covered directly and refrigerated. Return to room temperature before using.)
- Prepare the lasagna: Position the highest rack in the oven so that it sits about 6 inches below the top. Heat oven to 400 degrees.
- If tomato sauce, béchamel and ricotta filling are cold, bring to room temperature or warm them as needed.
- Set a large pot of water over high heat. Cover and bring to a boil. Set a large colander in a baking dish and place near stove.
- Season the boiling water generously with salt until it tastes like sea water. Carefully lay one sheet of pasta on the water's surface. Let it be completely immersed in the boiling water, using a slotted spoon to gently it push down if

needed, before adding the next sheet. Add two more pasta sheets in this way and cook for about 2 minutes, or until light in color, floppy in texture and completely cooked through. If pasta bubbles above the water's surface, use a slotted spoon to encourage it back in. Use a sieve to gently remove pasta from the water and into the prepared colander. Rinse under cold water until cool enough to handle, then begin assembly. Continue cooking, draining and rinsing pasta two or three sheets at a time as you assemble lasagna.

- Spoon about 3/4 cup béchamel into a 9-by-13-inch metal, glass or ceramic baking pan, and use a rubber spatula or your hands to generously coat bottom and sides of pan with sauce.

- Gently squeezing any remaining water from the pasta, use two or three sheets to entirely cover the bottom of the pan with minimal overlap, and leave ends hanging over sides. (They'll be helpful for sealing the top.) All four sides need not have overhang; two is plenty.

- Crumble about 1/3 of the ricotta mixture evenly over pasta to create foundation, then layer with sheets of pasta from edge to edge of pan. Use kitchen shears to help trim pasta to appropriate size and avoid overlap.

- Spread about 1/3 of the tomato sauce over next layer and cover with pasta.

- Spread about 1 cup béchamel evenly over next layer, sprinkle with 1/4 cup grated Parmesan, and cover with pasta.

- Repeat with remaining layers: ricotta, tomato sauce, béchamel and Parmesan, ricotta, tomato sauce, béchamel and Parmesan, following each with a layer of pasta. (If using thicker noodles, you might not be able to fit 8 layers of noodles in the pan. If using store-bought or dried pasta, you can skip the noodle layer between the ricotta and tomato sauce as needed to prevent the lasagna from stretching higher than the top of the pan.)

- For the top, fold overhanging pasta over a whole sheet to create a sealed pasta layer, then spread with remaining béchamel. Gently cover lasagna with a piece of parchment and wrap tightly with foil. Place onto a baking sheet to catch any overflow and bake on prepared rack.

- After 40 minutes, pull lasagna from oven and carefully remove foil and parchment. Sprinkle with grated mozzarella and return to oven until golden brown and bubbling on surface, about 20 minutes.

- Allow to cool for at least 15 minutes before slicing and serving. Leftover lasagna can be wrapped and refrigerated for up to 4 days. To freeze, bake 30 minutes but do not brown, then cool, and freeze for up to 4 weeks. Defrost, then sprinkle with mozzarella and bake uncovered at 400 degrees for 25 to 30 minutes until golden brown and bubbling on surface.

47. Tomato Alphabet Soup

Serving: 4 to 6 servings (about 8 cups) | Prep: | Cook: | Ready in: 50mins

Ingredients

- 2 tablespoons extra-virgin olive oil
- 3 tablespoons unsalted butter
- 1 medium yellow or red onion, finely chopped
- 2 garlic cloves, smashed
- Kosher salt and black pepper
- 1 medium carrot, chopped
- 1 rib celery, chopped
- 1 (28-ounce) can whole peeled tomatoes in juice
- 1 tablespoon tomato paste
- ½ to 1 cup alphabet pasta (or other very small shaped pasta), depending how hearty you like your soup

Direction

- Heat oil and 1 tablespoon butter in a heavy pot over medium heat. Stir in onion and garlic, season with salt and pepper, and cook, stirring often, until onions are softened, about 5 minutes.

- Stir in carrot and celery, and cook, stirring occasionally, until just tender, about 10 minutes.
- While the vegetables cook, strain the tomatoes over a bowl, separating the juice from the whole tomatoes, then squeeze the tomatoes over the liquid. Add the squeezed tomatoes and the tomato paste to the pot and cook, stirring frequently, until tomatoes start to caramelize, about 15 minutes.
- Meanwhile, cook the pasta in salted boiling water according to packing instructions. Reserve 1 cup of cooking liquid, strain, then return pasta to the pasta pot and gently stir in remaining 2 tablespoons butter; season to taste with salt and pepper and set aside.
- Add the tomato juices from the bowl and 2 cups water to the soup pot, stirring to scrape up any caramelized bits. Bring to a gentle simmer and cook, partly covered, until the vegetables are very tender, 10 to 15 minutes.
- Using an immersion or countertop blender, pureé the soup until very smooth. (If using a countertop blender, blend in batches with a kitchen towel over the lid of the blender.) Stir in pasta water as needed to thin soup to desired consistency. Stir in buttered alphabets and adjust seasoning. Divide among soup bowls.

48. Umami Garlic Noodles With Mustard Greens

Serving: 4 to 6 servings | Prep: | Cook: | Ready in: 45mins

Ingredients

- 4 large garlic cloves, finely grated or minced
- Kosher salt, as needed
- 10 ounces dried Chinese wheat noodles or Japanese ramen
- 1 tablespoon oyster sauce
- 2 teaspoons fish sauce
- 1 teaspoon cornstarch
- ½ teaspoon monosodium glutamate (MSG), or use 1/2 teaspoon chicken stock base or 2 tablespoons nutritional yeast
- ½ teaspoon granulated sugar
- 5 tablespoons salted, European-style (cultured) butter
- 10 ounces sliced shiitake or cremini mushrooms
- 1 large bunch mustard greens, stems and leaves, cut into 1 1/2-inch pieces
- Freshly ground black pepper
- 1 tablespoon minced shallot
- Chopped cilantro, for serving

Direction

- In a small bowl, cover garlic with 1 tablespoon water. Set aside.
- Bring a large pot of heavily salted water to a boil. Cook noodles 2 minutes less than package directions for very al dente. Reserve 3/4 cup noodle water, then drain noodles in a colander, rinse with cool water and set aside.
- In a small bowl, whisk together oyster sauce, fish sauce, cornstarch, MSG, sugar and reserved cooking water. Set aside.
- In a 12-inch skillet, melt 3 tablespoons butter over medium-high heat. Stir in mushrooms and cook until well browned, about 5 minutes. Stir in mustard greens and continue to cook, stirring frequently, until bright green and just tender, another 2 minutes. Turn off the heat, transfer to a bowl, and season with salt and pepper to taste.
- Return skillet to stove (with heat still off) and add remaining 2 tablespoons butter, shallot and garlic-water mixture (do not drain). As butter melts and sizzles, turn heat back on, to medium-low. Cook, stirring frequently, until garlic is fragrant and some pieces are golden, 3 to 5 minutes.
- Stir in cooking liquid mixture and raise heat to medium; bring sauce to a bubble. Using tongs, toss in noodles just until coated in sauce, then turn off heat. If noodles look too thick or taste too salty, add a splash of water. Stir in

mushrooms and mustard greens. Let it sit for 1 minute, then serve topped with cilantro.

Nutrition Information

- 319: calories;
- 1 gram: polyunsaturated fat;
- 34 grams: carbohydrates;
- 2 grams: dietary fiber;
- 10 grams: saturated fat;
- 5 grams: monounsaturated fat;
- 7 grams: protein;
- 1123 milligrams: sodium;
- 18 grams: fat;
- 0 grams: trans fat;
- 3 grams: sugars;

49. Vegan Lasagna

Serving: 8 servings | Prep: | Cook: | Ready in: 1hours15mins

Ingredients

- For the Sauce:
- 1 tablespoon olive oil
- 1 small white or yellow onion, chopped (about 1 cup)
- 2 garlic cloves, finely chopped
- 2 tablespoons tomato paste
- 1 teaspoon Italian seasoning (or 1 teaspoon dried oregano)
- ¼ teaspoon red-pepper flakes
- 1 (14-ounce) can diced tomatoes with their juices
- 1 (14-ounce) can crushed tomatoes
- 1 tablespoon vegan sugar (optional)
- Kosher salt, to taste
- For the Vegan Ricotta:
- 2 cups raw cashews
- 1 small garlic clove
- 3 tablespoons fresh lemon juice
- 1 (15-ounce) block extra-firm tofu, lightly pressed between paper towels to remove excess moisture
- 2 tablespoons nutritional yeast
- Kosher salt and black pepper
- For Assembly:
- Olive oil, for greasing
- Kosher salt
- 9 to 12 uncooked lasagna noodles
- Fresh basil leaves, for garnish (optional)

Direction

- Make the marinara sauce: Heat the olive oil in a pot over medium-high. Add the onion and cook, stirring often, until the onion is soft and translucent, 4 to 5 minutes. Add the garlic and cook, stirring constantly, for another minute. Stir in the tomato paste, Italian seasoning and red-pepper flakes, then stir in the diced and crushed tomatoes and sugar, if using. Allow the sauce to come to a simmer, then reduce the heat to low and cook for 5 minutes, uncovered. Add salt to taste. You can leave the sauce textured or purée it with an immersion blender, depending on your preference. Remove from heat.
- Make the ricotta: Add the cashews and garlic to a food processor and process until the cashews form a coarse meal, about 1 minute. Stop and scrape down the sides of the processor, then turn the processor back on. While it's running, drizzle in 1/2 cup water and the lemon juice. Process until completely smooth and the texture resembles hummus, another 2 minutes.
- Crumble the block of tofu into the processor, add the nutritional yeast, and season with salt and pepper. Continue processing until the mixture is smooth and resembles ricotta, stopping to scrape the sides of the processor as needed, about 1 minute. Taste and adjust salt and pepper.
- Assemble the lasagna: Heat the oven to 350 degrees and lightly oil a 9-by-13-inch casserole dish. Bring a large, salted pot of water to boil. Cook the lasagna noodles according to

package instructions, until they're al dente. (Skip this step if you're using no-boil noodles.)

- Layer 1 scant cup marinara sauce at the bottom of your lasagna dish. Cover it with a layer of 3 to 4 lasagna noodles. Cover the noodles with half the vegan ricotta. Cover the ricotta with another layer of noodles, followed by another cup of marinara and the remaining ricotta. Add a final layer of noodles and the remaining marinara sauce. Bake the lasagna for 40 to 45 minutes, or until the marinara on top is dark and the lasagna is bubbling. Top with torn basil leaves, if desired, and serve.

50. Vietnamese Rice Noodles With Lemongrass Shrimp

Serving: 4 servings | Prep: | Cook: | Ready in: 1hours

Ingredients

- For the pickled vegetables:
- 1 cup finely julienned carrot
- 1 cup finely julienned daikon
- 2 teaspoons granulated sugar
- ½ teaspoon salt
- 1 tablespoon rice vinegar
- For the dipping sauce:
- 3 tablespoons light brown sugar
- 3 tablespoons rice vinegar
- 4 tablespoons lime juice
- 3 tablespoons Vietnamese fish sauce, like Red Boat
- 3 garlic cloves, minced
- 1 tablespoon minced or grated ginger
- 1 medium-hot red chile pepper, such as Fresno, finely chopped
- 1 red or green bird chile pepper, thinly sliced, or substitute half a thinly sliced serrano pepper
- For the shrimp and noodles:
- 1 ½ pounds shrimp, preferably wild, peeled and deveined
- 2 tablespoons Vietnamese fish sauce

- 1 tablespoon light brown sugar
- 3 garlic cloves, minced
- 3 tablespoons finely chopped lemongrass, pale tender center part only
- 1 pound rice noodles, preferably rice vermicelli
- 1 or 2 small lettuce heads, with the leaves separated, rinsed and patted dry
- 3 cups mixed herb sprigs, such as cilantro, mint, basil, watercress and tender celery leaves
- 2 tablespoons vegetable oil
- 4 scallions, slivered
- 4 tablespoons crushed roasted peanuts
- Handful of bean sprouts (optional)

Direction

- Make the pickled vegetables: Put carrot and daikon in a small bowl and sprinkle with sugar and salt. Add rice vinegar, toss well and set aside.
- Make the dipping sauce: In a small bowl, stir together brown sugar, vinegar, lime juice, fish sauce, garlic, ginger and chiles. Stir in 1/2 cup cold water and let mixture sit for 15 minutes. (Leftover sauce will keep up to 3 days, refrigerated.)
- Marinate the shrimp: Put shrimp in a shallow dish. Add fish sauce, brown sugar, garlic and lemongrass. Mix well to coat.
- Meanwhile, bring a large pot of water to boil. Turn off heat and add rice noodles. Soak noodles, stirring occasionally, until softened, usually about 7 to 8 minutes. Drain and rinse with cold water. Leave in colander at room temperature.
- Prepare a platter of lettuce leaves and herb sprigs for the table. Keep cool, covered with a damp towel.
- Put oil in a wok or frying pan over medium-high heat. When oil is hot, add shrimp without crowding (work in batches if necessary). Cook for about 2 minutes per side, until lightly browned.
- To serve, divide noodles among 4 large soup bowls, then top each with hot shrimp, pickled vegetables and a tablespoon or so of dipping

sauce. Sprinkle with scallions and peanuts
(and beans sprouts if using). Pass herb platter
and remaining dipping sauce at the table, and
encourage guests to customize bowls as
desired.

Index

Conclusion

Thank you again for downloading this book!

I hope you enjoyed reading about my book!

If you enjoyed this book, please take the time to share your thoughts and post a review on Amazon. It'd be greatly appreciated!

Write me an honest review about the book – I truly value your opinion and thoughts and I will incorporate them into my next book, which is already underway.

Thank you!

If you have any questions, **feel free to contact at:** _author@thymerecipes.com_

Rachel Jones

thymerecipes.com

Printed in Great Britain
by Amazon